DownWRITE Funny

Using students' love of the ridiculous to build serious writing skills

Randy Larson

illustrated by

Judy Larson

Routledge
Taylor & Francis Group
NEW YORK AND LONDON

First published in 1997 by Prufrock Press Inc.

Published in 2021 by Routledge
605 Third Avenue, New York, NY 10017
2 Park Square, Milton Park, Abingdon, Oxon OX14 4RN

Routledge is an imprint of the Taylor & Francis Group, an informa business.

Copyright © 1997 by Taylor & Francis Group.

Notice:
Product or corporate names may be trademarks or registered trademarks, and are used only for identification and explanation without intent to infringe.

ISBN-13: 978-1-0321-4181-7 (hbk)
ISBN-13: 978-1-8776-7331-3 (pbk)

DOI: : 10.4324/9781003234715

Introduction

My wife Judy and I have worked hard to make *DownWRITE Funny* a book that will reach today's young people. The illustrations and the activities are a bit zany and offbeat, certainly not the kind of thing found in most textbooks. The illustrations are designed to work hand in hand with the text and open the door for teaching important concepts about writing.

One assumption underlying *DownWRITE Funny* is that students today are not just bored with school—they are annoyed. Who can blame them when you consider all the dry, humorless textbooks written by committees, textbooks that are drained of all life and color in an attempt to do everything, to please everyone and to offend no one?

Another assumption is that students today are part of a visual generation. They watch gobs of television shows and stacks of DVDs. They surf the Internet and play Nintendo. They sometimes go to a favorite movie not once or twice but eight or nine times. Like it or not, they are often more comfortable with pictures than with words. *DownWRITE Funny* capitalizes on this, melding visual images with text to teach fundamental writing skills.

When students receive an activity from *DownWRITE Funny*, they know they have something different in their hands. The illustrations and assignments appeal to their sense of the ridiculous. I know that when I give my students an assignment from *DownWRITE Funny*, they pay attention. A cartoon of a baby winged hippopotamus being helped back into its nest is just strange enough to make them sit up and take notice. When the accompanying assignment is challenging and interesting to do, my 7th–12th graders work hard at it. They appreciate activities and exercises designed especially for them. More important, the activities get them involved in working to become better writers.

Using *DownWRITE Funny*. As a teacher, you can drop *DownWRITE Funny* activities on students in small doses. Or you might use an activity to introduce a concept, rather like showing a cartoon before the main attraction. However, you will realize the most positive results when you use *DownWRITE Funny* on a regular basis.

That's why, in most sections of the book, you will see several pages devoted to one writing skill. There are three activities devoted to run-on sentences, for example, and three devoted to using specific words. Students thus have several chances to master a skill, without getting bored. Each activity challenges them to use their imaginations as they learn how to become more effective writers.

There is joy in the writing process. There is humor and fun and challenge. Judy and I hope that you and your students experience all of these and more as you work together on activities that are *DownWRITE Funny*.

Randy Larson

Common Core State Standards Alignment Sheet
DownWrite Funny

All lessons in this book align to the following standards.

Grade Level	Common Core State Standards in ELA-Literacy
Grade 5	L.5.1 Demonstrate command of the conventions of standard English grammar and usage when writing or speaking. L.5.2 Demonstrate command of the conventions of standard English capitalization, punctuation, and spelling when writing. L.5.3 Use knowledge of language and its conventions when writing, speaking, reading, or listening. L.5.5 Demonstrate understanding of figurative language, word relationships, and nuances in word meanings. W.5.4 Produce clear and coherent writing in which the development and organization are appropriate to task, purpose, and audience. W.5.5 With guidance and support from peers and adults, develop and strengthen writing as needed by planning, revising, editing, rewriting, or trying a new approach. (Editing for conventions should demonstrate command of Language standards 1-3 up to and including grade 5 here.)
Grade 6	L.6.1 Demonstrate command of the conventions of standard English grammar and usage when writing or speaking. L.6.2 Demonstrate command of the conventions of standard English capitalization, punctuation, and spelling when writing. L.6.3 Use knowledge of language and its conventions when writing, speaking, reading, or listening. W.6.4 Produce clear and coherent writing in which the development, organization, and style are appropriate to task, purpose, and audience. W.6.5 With some guidance and support from peers and adults, develop and strengthen writing as needed by planning, revising, editing, rewriting, or trying a new approach. (Editing for conventions should demonstrate command of Language standards 1–3 up to and including grade 6 here.)
Grade 7	L.7.1 Demonstrate command of the conventions of standard English grammar and usage when writing or speaking. L.7.2 Demonstrate command of the conventions of standard English capitalization, punctuation, and spelling when writing. L.7.3 Use knowledge of language and its conventions when writing, speaking, reading, or listening. W.7.4 Produce clear and coherent writing in which the development, organization, and style are appropriate to task, purpose, and audience. W.7.5 With some guidance and support from peers and adults, develop and strengthen writing as needed by planning, revising, editing, rewriting, or trying a new approach, focusing on how well purpose and audience have been addressed. (Editing for conventions should demonstrate command of Language standards 1–3 up to and including grade 7 here.)
Grade 8	L.8.1 Demonstrate command of the conventions of standard English grammar and usage when writing or speaking. L.8.2 Demonstrate command of the conventions of standard English capitalization, punctuation, and spelling when writing. L.8.3 Use knowledge of language and its conventions when writing, speaking, reading, or listening. W.8.4 Produce clear and coherent writing in which the development, organization, and style are appropriate to task, purpose, and audience. W.8.5 With some guidance and support from peers and adults, develop and strengthen writing as needed by planning, revising, editing, rewriting, or trying a new approach, focusing on how well purpose and audience have been addressed. (Editing for conventions should demonstrate command of Language standards 1–3 up to and including grade 8 here.)

Table of Contents

Writing
Activities

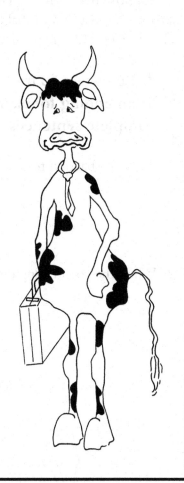

Fragment Frustration

Sentence fragments frustrate people. That's because fragments don't finish the thoughts they start.

Suppose that someone comes up to you and says, "Tonight after school." If that's all the person says, you will probably be frustrated. You will find yourself thinking, "Tonight after school, *WHAT?*" You will want the message to be finished.

★ Below are 12 frustrating sentence fragments. Write a beginning or an ending for each fragment. Be sure that you end up with 12 complete sentences that make sense.

1. After the balloon toss

_____

_____

2. When the coyote king died

_____

_____

3. When I came upon the scene

_____

_____

4. By the time it was over

_____

_____

5. When she eats pizza

_____

_____

6. When the medicine kicked in

_____

_____

7. Along about midnight

_____

_____

8. Near the exit

_____

_____

9. Next to her brother Jake

_____

_____

10. Because of the principal's cat

_____

_____

11. Because of everything she had done for the past 16 years

_____

_____

12. Beneath the muddy water of Silver Lake near the town of Hackensack where my mother and her ex-husband live

_____

_____

★ Write a story using at least 6 of the sentences you have completed, above. This won't be easy! Feel free to mix up the order of the sentences. You may also add extra words or even entire sentences.

Complete Thoughts

A sentence is a complete thought. That doesn't mean that a sentence tells you absolutely everything there is to know about a subject. It means that it doesn't leave you hanging.

Imagine that newspaper reporters wrote in sentence fragments, instead of complete sentences. You might end up reading an article like this:

> **Des Moines, Iowa.** Today an accident. Because it was inflated. After the snake slid by. By the skin of her teeth. In the danger zone. Other than french fries.

A story like this raises more questions than it answers. It won't make a bit of sense until each thought is completed.

★ **Complete the thoughts in the article above so that the story makes sense. Make sure that your finished story has no sentence fragments.**

_____

_____

_____

_____

_____

_____

_____

★ **Rewrite each sentence fragment below so that it makes a complete sentence.**

1. The boxing bunnies at the side of the road

   _____

   _____

2. Not without fruitcake

   _____

   _____

3. In the ditch

   _____

   _____

4. Completely insane

   _____

   _____

5. Because she was only seven feet tall

   _____

   _____

6. Other than beef sandwiches

   _____

   _____

7. Before they invented pencils

   _____

   _____

8. In the golden mist of sunset

   _____

   _____

No Jamming

Each sentence you write carries a message. However, when one sentence runs into another, and then into another and another, the messages get jammed together, like luggage at an airport baggage claim. A pile of suitcases is hard to sort out. So is a pile of sentences. Sentences that are jammed together without proper punctuation are called run-on sentences.

★ **Sort out the run-on sentences below. Place a capital letter at the beginning of each sentence and a period, question mark or exclamation point at the end of each sentence.**

On Goldfish Pond

Little Elsie was feeding the two-foot long white goldfish in the pond at the Castle Hotel her family stayed there every time her father went to the annual Disgruntled Postal Workers Convention in Iowa Elsie liked the hotel because of the big fish under the fake drawbridge that led to the fake castle where all the guests slept.

As Elsie was feeding the big goldfish pieces of a sweet roll from the free continental breakfast by the fake swimming pool, she was startled by a tall man dressed like a knight and his red-haired friend, who were both carrying luggage for people out to their cars she accidentally dropped the whole sweet roll into the pond, and the goldfish churned up the water trying to get at it one elderly lady got scared and ran into the castle screaming, "Sharks sharks" the manager raced outside to see what she was talking about and somehow knocked the redhead into the water the redhead started yelling, "I'm allergic to fish they'll kill me they'll kill me!"

A guest on the fourth floor heard the screaming and tossed out ten bed sheets tied together to make a rope he yelled, "hang on" the redhead hung on and was pulled 30 feet into the air, but just as he was about to be pulled to safety through the window, the sheets ripped he fell like a stone on top of

Reminder:
A sentence is a group of words that has a subject and a verb *and* communicates a complete thought. It begins with a capital letter and ends with an appropriate punctuation mark.

the knight, who was carrying duffel bags for sixteen fishermen in town for a carp derby the knight toppled into the pond, almost drowning the elderly lady she had come back outside, slipped on a stray piece of sweet roll and fallen into the pond she was now treading water and screaming at the redhead it was lucky that the knight had air bag underwear because the underwear blew up upon collision with the pond the woman, the redhead and the knight were all three able to drift six feet to "shore," where the visiting fishermen were standing one turned to the crowd and said, "get me the net, boys one of those is a keeper."

★ **What happened next? Continue the story in another short paragraph of your own. Be sure that your sentences are separate and clear.**

No Jumbling

People can do strange things to sentences. Sometimes they leave out the subject. Sometimes they leave out the verb. Sometimes they don't finish their thought. Sometimes they jam too many thoughts into one sentence and wind up with what is known as a run-on sentence.

In a run-on sentence, there aren't enough capital letters or punctuation marks to tell readers when one thought has finished and another has begun. A run-on sentence should be separated into two or more sentences.

★ **The paragraph below contains both simple, clear sentences and run-on sentences. Untangle the run-ons by putting in the necessary end punctuation marks and by adding capital letters wherever they are needed.**

Cat psychiatrists are busy these days because the stress placed upon pet cats has increased people come home from work after a two-hour ride on the freeway and pet cats demand attention as soon as humans open the door a pet cat is supposed to act fascinated and start purring it doesn't matter to anyone that maybe the cat has been having a bad hairball day the cat's feelings are totally ignored it's only the whiny little humans that have real problems after a few months of this treatment, most cats need therapy without it they often end up on the streets pushing a grocery cart and looking for pigeons that have bad coughs.

★ The paragraph below consists of one long run-on sentence about Armadillo Lil, a woman with a taste for chili dogs and a fondness for acrobatic reptiles. Break the run-on sentence into three complete sentences. Place capital letters where they belong, and insert the proper end punctuation marks.

Armadillo Lil had a food stand that advertised a foot-long chili dog and fries for one dollar of course it was always crowded, which gave Lil a chance to show off her well-trained reptiles: an alligator, a snake, a turtle the size of a cantaloupe and a collection of Arizona lizards that did a great little trapeze act everything was fine until a stranger in a cowboy hat approached Lil's stand and accused her of selling "reptile chili."

★ Finish the story about Lil. In completing the story, be sure not to write any run-on sentences of your own.

Starting and Stopping

Throwing sentences together without starting points (capital letters) and stopping points (periods, question marks or exclamation points) is like presenting someone with a huge cream pie and saying, "Okay, dig in!"—but without giving him a fork, a knife or a plate. Pie eaters do better with tools to help them out, just as readers do better with tools to help them out. Sentences jammed together without punctuation and capital letters are called run-on sentences. They need to be separated from each other with capital letters, periods, question marks and exclamation points.

★ **The story below is full of run-on sentences. Read through it and decide where the individual sentences begin and end. Insert capital letters and end punctuation marks where needed. You may have to cross out a few words here and there to make the sentences clear and readable.**

The room was chilly when Rodney finally woke up a shrill beep had been echoing in his dream for the past 20 minutes, but he couldn't force himself to open his eyes finally he did the curtains were blowing across his desk but the window was closed a sharp blue light filled the room when he turned back the covers of his bed ten red Christmas tree ornaments with black legs marched up onto his pillow and started singing, "How Much Is That Doggie in the Window?" then Rodney got scared he ran to the door but it disappeared as he touched the knob a voice said, "If you like tuna-melt sandwiches, follow us" Rodney followed the little red people took him to a big sweaty warehouse filled with tables of cold cuts and wheat bread and tubs of tuna and the red creatures told him they were catering a UFO reunion to be held in Herbie Wartz's UFO Repair Shop on Thursday and if Rodney wanted to come all he had to do was show up suddenly the moon came out and beamed so brightly into his eyes that he had to dive back into bed and cover up his head and he didn't wake up until Thursday he thought he'd had a nightmare until he saw tuna-melt crumbs on his pillow right then and there he decided to go to Herbie's UFO Repair Shop and check things out.

★ Continue the story. Tell what happens after Rodney visits his UFO pal, Herbie Wartz. Be careful not to write any run-on sentences.

Straightforward and Simple

Sentences written in the **active voice** are direct, straightforward and simple in design. They are almost always more effective than sentences written in the **passive voice.**

Here is a sentence written in the **active voice:**

Angela tossed the fruitcake out the window.

"Angela" is the subject, which comes first. She is the "do-er"—the one performing the action of tossing. This same sentence written in the **passive voic**e would read like this:

The fruitcake was tossed out the window by Angela.

Now "fruitcake" is the subject of the sentence. The fruitcake isn't *doing* anything. It is *receiving* the action. It is being tossed.

In active sentences, the subject of the sentence comes first and performs the action of the sentence. Here is another example of an active sentence:

Hector threw sand at the camera.

"Hector" is the subject. He comes first and performs the action of throwing. The same sentence, written in the **passive voice,** would read like this:

The camera was thrown sand at by Hector.

Now the subject of the sentence is "camera," but the camera isn't *doing* anything. Hector is. The sentence sounds slow, confusing and awkward.

Avoid writing passive sentences. Generally, writing is much easier to understand when the subject of the sentence performs the action.

DOI: 10.4324/9781003234715-3

★ Rewrite the passive sentences below into active sentences.

1. Cindersmella was searched for by the Prince of Slippers.

2. The lemon was squeezed by an elf named Louise.

3. Home was phoned by the last lonely alien.

★ Using only active sentences, explain what is happening (or is about to happen) in the illustration above.

Active and Clear

Sentences written in the active voice are almost always clearer than sentences written in the passive voice. In an active sentence the subject is right up front and performs the action. Here's one example:

Alphonse wrenched the sucker from his toothless gums and said, "Thith hath got to thtop!"

In the passive voice, the subject *receives* the action performed in the sentence, like this:

The sucker was wrenched from his toothless gums by Alphonse, who then said, "Thith hath got to thtop!"

★ **Rewrite the following passive sentences into active sentences.**

1. Short buildings were leaped over by Emilio using a trampoline.

_____

_____

2. Mr. Mavin's bald head was rubbed by the genie.

_____

_____

3. Waiting for Louise on the front porch was the door-to-door plunger salesman.

_____

_____

4. *Space Rodents In Love* was made a hit movie by children who love its weird humor.

_____

_____

5. The expired cereal box tops were saved by Ms. Wopper.

_____

★ **Read the story below and mark an *A* next to the *active* sentences and a *P* next to the *passive* ones.**

_____ Throughout the long, dark Halloween night, a complete buffalo costume was worn by Billie Beaker. _____ He started his evening by gallumphing up to Mrs. Johnson's door and bellowing in his best buffalo impersonation, "Trick or treat!"

_____ The door was opened by Mrs. Johnson. _____ Lawn clippings were dropped into Billie's sack by her.

_____ Billie went away feeling sad. _____ He moaned deeply and sorrowfully. _____ Just then, a real buffalo at the edge of town heard him.

_____ At Mrs. Humblepup's house ten minutes later, something bumped Billie on the neck. _____ He whirled around. _____ A seven-foot buffalo stared down at him with bulging eyes full of buffalo sympathy and understanding. _____ A scream was launched into the cold night air by Billie. _____ He raced through Mrs. Humblepup's garden, flattening her scarecrow on the way out.

_____ The sight of glowing buffalo eyes was never forgotten by Billie. _____ The night light was kept on in his room until he was 18 years old.

★ **Now, on a separate sheet of paper, rewrite the passive sentences above into active ones.**

To the Point

Healthy sentences are active. They put the subject right up front, and the subject performs the action in the sentence. An example:

Edith slipped on some tapioca pudding, slid off the porch and hit her head.

In a passive sentence, the subject *receives* the action instead of performing it. The sentence above would sound like this in the passive voice:

Edith's head was hit after she slipped on some tapioca pudding and slid off the porch.

The first sentence, written in the active voice, is much clearer and to the point. The active voice is almost always easier to understand than the passive voice.

★ **Rewrite the two passive sentences below into active sentences.**

1. A bench was sat on by Humpty Dumpty's great-grandson.

_____

_____

_____

2. He was looked for by a large, demented chicken.

_____

_____

_____

★ **Rewrite the passive sentences below into active sentences.**

Applause was given by the audience as the stage was appeared on by Madam Zorrino.

The call for a volunteer was answered by Abby Tweed. Placed into the Super Human

Activator Device by Madam Zorrino was Abby's hand. Its breath was held by the audience.

The crank on the machine was spun furiously by Madam Zorrino.

★ **Finish the story of Madam Zorrino by adding five active sentences of your own.**

On Purpose

People write for many different reasons. *How* and *what* they write depends upon their purpose in writing.

> ★ **Look at the sentences below. Each one was written with a different purpose—to** *beg, scare, teach, entertain, encourage, comfort* **or** *invite*. **Determine the purpose intended for each sentence and write the purpose on the line provided.**

1. _____ How can you say you have no brains? Your head is as big as a pumpkin, honey.

2. _____ If you crack three eggs into a bowl, beat the mixture to a froth, then apply it to your head with a cheese knife, your hairdo will last for almost two and a half years.

3. _____ If you get caught chewing gum, they will take you down into the boiler room and make you drink dishwater from the cafeteria.

4. _____ I'm having a party Saturday night, and I sure wish you would come—dressed in something washable.

5. _____ About midnight at our family reunion, we heard someone shouting, "Take that, you little monsters!" We ran to the tent next door to find Uncle Zachary leaping over sleeping bags, trying to swat mosquitoes with Aunt Lorna's wig. I laughed so hard I fell into a tent pole and collapsed the whole thing.

6. _____ If you let me go to camp, I'll scrub your tennis racket with a toothbrush, keep Toby out of your bath tub and take my vitamins every night for the rest of my life.

7. _____ You can run the three-legged race and win because you have three legs! Go out there and give it your all!

DownWrite Funny © Taylor & Francis   DOI: 10.4324/9781003234715-4

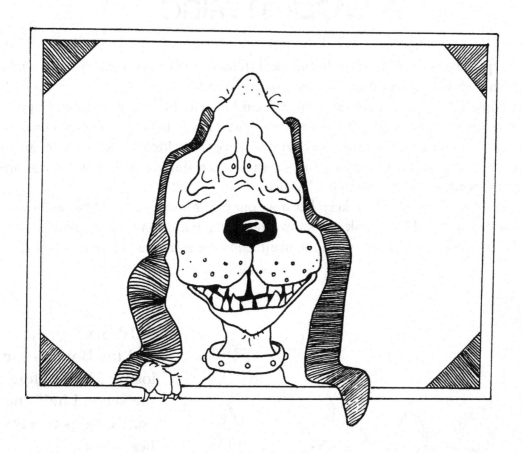

★ You are a basset hound with a personal problem. You haven't had a date in two years (or 14 dog years).

You have decided it's time to advertise. Write up an ad for the "Date Me" section of the *Beagle Bugle*. Tell only those things about yourself that will help accomplish your *purpose*, which is to find a mate.

A Goal in Mind

In both speaking and writing, people choose different words in different circumstances. The words they choose often depend on their *goal* or *purpose*.

For example, if a boy asks his older sister to help him with his science project, he might flatter her by saying, "You're so good at this stuff, Stacy. If you help me, my project will be so much better. Besides, we'll get to spend more time together. Pretty soon you're going to be off at college, and we'll hardly ever get to see each other. But if you help me on this project, I'll get to spend quality time with my big sister."

If the boy's goal is to get her to keep her nose out of his business, he might say, "Get your own science project! You think you know everything, but I don't see any science trophies with *your* name on them sitting on the mantle. Do me a favor and leave me alone!"

★ It's half-time, and the Bobcats are losing 53–3. Before the second half, the coach wants to talk to her players.

Below are the opening lines for five possible half-time speeches by the coach. What is the purpose behind each opening line?

1. I'm sorry for being such a lousy coach. I feel I've let you all down.

   Purpose: _____

2. We're only 50 points behind. Come on. That's not so bad!

   Purpose: _____

3. It's not the score that sizzles my bacon. It's the way you people are playing out there!

   Purpose: _____

4. Remember, when you shoot, dribble once, fake with the head and then release the ball.

   Purpose: _____

5. For every basket you make, I'll bake you a brownie.

   Purpose: _____

   ★ **Now choose *one* of the opening lines above and finish the coach's speech. Be sure your words keep the coach's purpose in mind.**

   _____

   _____

   _____

   _____

   _____

   _____

   _____

   _____

   _____

   _____

   _____

   _____

   _____

No Accidents

Every piece of writing has a purpose—to kill time, to record daily miseries, to remind yourself to pick up milk at the store, to get an *A* from Ms. Winksniffer in English 101—or a zillion other purposes. The trick is to *accomplish* your purpose when you write.

Suppose you are a teacher whose purpose is to help students understand the anatomy of the human heart. However, everyone who reads your handout forgets about veins and arteries and starts thinking about those little heart candies sold around Valentine's Day. You haven't accomplished your purpose.

Suppose you are a boy whose purpose is to ask a girl out on a date. She reads your note, thinks it's about a math problem you are having trouble with and offers you a lesson in dividing improper fractions. You haven't accomplished your purpose.

Always keep purpose on your mind when you write. Always.

Look at the illustration of the mad scientist on the next page. What could she possibly have to say to a roomful of Frankenstein monsters? What could be her purpose? Perhaps it is one of the following:

- **Purpose #1.** It's graduation day at Monster University. Ms. Mad Scientist is informing the Frankenstein graduates of the career opportunities that await them.

- **Purpose #2.** Ms. Mad Scientist is trying to lift the spirits of a group of monsters with poor self-images. The monsters think they are ugly and unwanted.

- **Purpose #3.** Ms. Mad Scientist is seeking donations for her next big experiment. The monsters will be encouraged to donate time, money or themselves to the project.

- **Purpose #4.** Ms. Mad Scientist is at a Scientists Anonymous meeting and is detailing her own story of science addiction.

- **Purpose #5.** Ms. Mad Scientist is explaining to the monsters her plan for using them to conquer the world.

- **Purpose #6.** Ms. Mad Scientist is trying to make the monsters laugh by doing her stand-up comedy routine.

★ Choose one of the purposes listed on the previous page. Then write a speech for **Ms. Mad Scientist** that accomplishes that purpose.

The Changing Audience

A writer's **audience** changes from day to day, from subject to subject, from situation to situation.

One day you might write an article for the school newspaper about the best way to interview for summer jobs. Your audience would be your classmates.

The next day, you might send a letter to the Dead Duck Dogfood Company complaining about the terrible odor that filled your home as soon as you opened the bag. In this case, your audience would be the owners of the company.

On the weekend, you might write a thank-you note for the money Grandma Hazel sent for your birthday. Your audience, of course, would be your grandmother.

★ **Who is the intended audience for each statement below?**
Briefly describe the audience on the line provided.

1. Selling Sappy Sucker vacuum cleaners is your ticket to the future. Go get 'em!

Audience: _____

2. This is a robbery. Hand over all the money in the till, along with a box of Pampers.

Audience: _____

DOI: 10.4324/9781003234715-5

3. I want a Sluggo doll, a Vegetable Man and a box of 576 electronic Crayons. I'll leave cookies and milk on the table by the sofa. Love, Margie.

Audience: _____

4. Christmas List: gas mask—cousin Albert; kite—Jamie; electric socks—Grandpa Phil; dill pickles—Dad.

Audience: _____

5. Please allow my son back into Camp Duckwaddle. He's a good boy, and we've taken away his Mr. Magic Electric Shocker. Thank you.

Audience: _____

6. You are my sunshine, my moonlight, my angel of love and tenderness.

Audience: _____

7. All members are encouraged to keep their Captain Kirk uniforms on during the entire flight simulation.

Audience: _____

8. Please applaud when you see the APPLAUSE sign light up.

Audience: _____

9. Anyone involved in the incident must report to Ms. Hippleman by noon or be suspended.

Audience: _____

10. After you have removed the diaper, wrap it tightly in a plastic bag and deposit it in an air-tight container.

Audience: _____

Working Together

Writing is like dancing. The writer leads, and the audience gracefully follows. But if the writer leads in a certain direction and then switches abruptly, the audience stumbles. The rhythm is broken, and the audience is confused.

For example, suppose that a novelist sets out to write a mystery meant to entertain his readers. Halfway through the book he begins describing all of the poisonous plants in the world. He loses track of the story and winds up writing a science lesson about plants. Understandably, his readers will feel confused and cheated.

A skilled writer keeps in mind her **purpose** for writing *and* her intended **audience**. Then her writing will be clear, and her audience will never be confused.

★ **Name a possible *audience* and a possible *purpose* for the following books. In other words, *who* is the writer writing for and *why*?**

1. *Sixteen Ways to Milk a Dairy Goat*

   Audience: _____   Purpose: _____

2. *The Haunted Computer of Hapwick High*

   Audience: _____   Purpose: _____

3. *Living with a Teenager*

   Audience: _____   Purpose: _____

★ **Now write a book title for the following audiences and purposes.**

4. Book Title: _____

   Audience: E.R. nurses.   Purpose: to entertain

5. Book Title: _____

   Audience: Barbie doll collectors.   Purpose: to provide a guide to prices

6. Book Title: _____

   Audience: 60–80-year-old rock climbers. Purpose: to promote rock climbing for older adults

★ Examine this illustration and complete the following:

1. Describe the *audience* in the scene.

2. Describe what you think is the *purpose* of the piece of writing being read aloud.

3. Write a few lines of the story, poem or article being read.

Just the "Write" Magazine

Over 15,000 magazines are published in the United States every month, each one for a different audience. There are magazines for dental hygiene professionals, people who love wooden boats, roofers, people who live in the Milwaukee area, rug-hookers, model railroad fanatics, Civil War enthusiasts, yoga teachers, people who like spicy foods, people of Ukrainian heritage, owners of reptiles and amphibians, hot air balloon enthusiasts and hundreds of other groups. All of the magazines have one thing in common: They are written with a very specific audience in mind.

The writers write to please that audience. If they don't please the audience, the magazines won't sell. Then everyone at the magazine will be out of a job.

Imagine a magazine called *CaliCOOL*. The audience profile might read like this: *CaliCOOL* is a magazine written for very intelligent 4–10-year-old calico cats. The typical reader is an indoor calico cat with a collar. She is fed canned food and is slightly overweight—but still active, playful and frisky. She is well-trained, well-loved, sleeps more than 14 hours a day and purrs a lot.

The table of contents might include the following articles:

- A Rare Breed of Calico Reveals All. Carlos, one of the few male calicos in existence, poignantly reveals the pain and joy of being a minority among calicos.

- Collars that Grab Attention: A look at the latest in cat collars and tips about what colors are best for calicos.

- Coping with a Neglectful Owner: Three calico cats share three very different approaches to solving the problem of an owner who doesn't pamper his cat enough.

- An excerpt from *Uppity Cats Unite*, by award-winning author Cali Belle DiPrince. In this controversial book, DiPrince attacks the old-fashioned notion that people are the masters of cats.

- Salmon and Tuna and Sardines, Oh My: A new health study looks at how fattening some brands of fishy cat food can be.

Male calico tells **his** story

Fashion preview: The latest in cat collars

How do you cope with a **neglectful** owner?

★ Invent your own specialized magazine and write an audience profile that describes the typical readers of the publication. The profile should include basic information about the readers' age, income, education, hobbies, cultural background, family background, etc. Remember that the profile is a *general* profile, applying to a large share of the readers, not every single one of them.

After describing the audience, name the magazine, sketch the cover and list five articles for the table of contents. Be sure that the titles cover topics that will be of interest to the targeted audience.

Name of magazine: _____

Audience profile: _____

_____

_____

Table of contents:

1. _____

_____

2. _____

_____

_____

3. _____

_____

_____

4. _____

_____

_____

5. _____

_____

_____

Revealing Attitude

People don't usually speak in the flat voices of a recorded telephone message from directory assistance. They put *attitude* into their speech, stressing certain words and syllables to get their meaning across. This attitude is also referred to as *tone*.

For example, you may have heard a father warn his son, "Don't use that tone with me!" That usually happens after the son has said some perfectly acceptable words—but in a tone that makes his father want to ground him for a month. Someone can say "thanks a lot" and sound grateful and sincere, or sarcastic and bitter. The same words can have very different meaning, depending on the tone used.

Writers use tone, too. Since they can't emphasize certain words with their voices, they must do it by choosing their words carefully. To adopt a loving tone, they might use gentle words like "honey," "darling," "sweetheart" and "please." For an angry tone, they might use harsh words like "jerk" or "idiot," and demanding words like "Get out now!"

The tone of a piece of writing should always match the purpose of the writing. A loving, gentle tone doesn't make any sense if your purpose is to complain to the lawn care company that killed every piece of vegetation for three blocks. A business-like, impersonal tone doesn't make any sense if your purpose is to convince the love of your life to elope with you.

Reminder:

You must be ready to change your tone if it is damaging to your purpose. Don't scream on paper at a coach you think has treated you unfairly if you ever want to play on his team again. Don't write calmly about how "nice" a present was if it was the best gift you ever, ever, ever hope to receive in your lifetime. Make your tone fit your purpose.

DownWrite Funny © Taylor & Francis

DOI: 10.4324/9781003234715-6

★ Holly Hacker wants to write a letter to the Oatmeal Computer Company. What tone is she likely to take toward the manufacturer of her new computer? Angry? Pleading? Cool, calm and professional? Hysterical? Critical? Humorous?

Before you decide for sure, consider her purpose. Does she want a full refund? Does she want revenge? Does she want her computer repaired?

What is the best tone for her to use in order to accomplish her purpose?

After you decide the tone and purpose, write a letter for Holly to the Oatmeal Computer Company. (Note: Use no foul language or voodoo curses. She's mad, but not *that* mad.)

The Writer's Attitude

Writers adopt different tones for different purposes. For example, in a note to your best friend who moved away, you probably wouldn't say: *In reference to your last letter, I did indeed complete my algebra course with barely adequate grades, despite my dislike for the instructor.* The tone is too stuffy. You would be much more likely to adopt a casual, friendly tone and write something like this: *Oh, you asked about that stupid algebra class. I did pass, but just barely. It's a miracle, since you know how I can't stand Mrs. Carbunkle.*

Read the four short paragraphs below about a girl named Marcy Maples. Each paragraph has a different *tone*.

Friendly/Conversational Tone

Imagine buying 25 pairs of pink *elephants!* Marcy did, and she shipped the whole kit-and-kaboodle off to her mother for Christmas. You gotta love this kid for her weird taste!

Formal Tone

According to our records, Ms. Marcy Maples, on December 22 of last year, forwarded a package from this office to a Ms. Gladys Maples in Elk Tooth, Alaska. The package was received in Elk Tooth on December 27 and signed for by a Mr. Elvin Maples at 2:00 PM.

Hysterical Tone

This is the most insane thing any half-witted person could do! Marcy Maples shipped 25 pairs of hot pink elephants to her mother, who lives somewhere in the middle of Alaska. Miss Marcy should be locked up in a mental ward!

Critical Tone

It would take someone without much intelligence to send her mother a clumsy, ill-packed box of elephants for Christmas. People should have more sense. Who does Marcy Maples think she is?

★ Herbert Harrison was kicked out of Camp
Duckwaddle for pulling a practical joke on his camp counselor. Write
four different letters to four different people about what happened:

- Make one letter *friendly* in tone.
- Use a *formal* tone in another letter.
- Give one letter a *hysterical* tone.
- Make one letter *critical* in tone.

Decide on the purpose of each letter before you begin. (Is it to complain, to share a funny story, to threaten? Or is it for some other purpose?)
Who is writing the letter, and to whom?

Just a few ideas: Herbert might write to his parents. The counselor
might write to the camp director. Herbert's roommate might write to his
friends. The counselor's lawyer might write to Herbert's parents.

Diplomacy Counts

Diplomacy often involves using words that don't hurt or embarrass quite so much. For example, if you want to tell your coach that she has bad breath, you don't say, "Your breath smells like you just ate dog food." Instead, you might say, "Would you like to try one of my breath mints, Ms. Muckle? They're yummy!"

Practicing diplomacy spares people's feelings. It also keeps you from being friendless! Here are some examples:

Not diplomatic	Diplomatic
• I've never met a person as rude as you.	• You certainly know how to come straight to the point.
• When was the last time you took a bath? You stink!	• Would you like to try this free sample of "Fresh-as-a-Daisy" bubble bath?
• If you were any stupider, you'd be a shoelace.	• You have a wonderful grasp of the simple things in life.

★ **Now it's your turn. Change the critical words below into more diplomatic phrases.**

1. When you smile, I lose my appetite.

   _____

   _____

2. If I were your neighbor, I'd move.

   _____

   _____

3. Those pimples look like serious volcanoes ready to explode.

   _____

   _____

4. You have the personality of a turnip.

   _____

   _____

"Manfred, I think it would be best if we started seeing other reptiles," Betty said as she slid heavily into the bog.

★ Betty and Manfred have been dating for six months. They have shared many bug-snacks together and have swum a lot of bogs. However, things have become tense in the last few weeks. Betty has decided she wants her "space." She wants to swim new swamps and go to night school. As she leaves Manfred on the shore, he calls out to her, "What have I done that's so terrible?"

Betty decides to take some time with her answer and e-mail it to Manfred later. Write Betty's reply using all the gentle diplomacy you can. Don't crush Manfred with harsh words. Let Betty tell Manfred honestly—but gently—why he is not the lizard for her. Write about Manfred's bad habits without making him feel like a complete lizard loser.

Smoothing the Way

When sentences and paragraphs sound choppy and disconnected, a writer has probably failed to use *transitional expressions* (often called *transitions*). Transitions help readers go smoothly from one idea to another. They can be placed at the beginning, in the middle or at the end of sentences.

Some of the most common transitional expressions are listed in the box below.

---

although • after • afterward • also • and • because • before • besides
but • eventually • finally • first • however • meanwhile •on the other hand
next • similarly • since • then • therefore • today • unless • until • while

---

★ **Read the story below and circle all the transitional expressions.**

The Princess and the Squash

Lady Myrtle's little pet dragon Maynard had been dragging his tail ever since the drawbridge accident, so she decided to perk him up by putting him to work. Because it was such a beautiful, leaf-scented spring day, she decided he should come outside and help her plant a garden.

First, Maynard waddled ahead of her, making nifty furrows in the soft dirt with his damaged tail. Then Lady Myrtle, addicted to turnips and full of joy, waltzed behind, casting seed onto the ground in neat, zippy rows.

There was a problem, however. Lady Myrtle soon saw that she couldn't wear her slippers in the garden because it was so muddy. Sir Bernie often came up to the fence by the garden, hoping that someone would offer him a free squash. The problem? Everyone knew that if a knight saw a lady's bare feet, he would have to propose marriage—whether he loved her or not.

DownWrite Funny © Taylor & Francis   DOI: 10.4324/9781003234715-7

On this particular spring day, Lady Myrtle saw no sign of Sir Bernie, so she took off her slippers and continued planting. While she worked, though, Sir Bernie walked up to the fence and leaned against it, dreaming of luscious vegetables. Maynard sensed his presence and started growling. Lady Myrtle, who didn't know what was wrong at first, put Maynard on his leash.

Since Maynard hated knights, his nostrils started to flare. Red smoke wafted up in the form of a smoky little flame that didn't scare anybody. Lady Myrtle jerked on Maynard's leash, causing him to hiccup and shoot an arc of flame in Sir Bernie's direction. Immediately the scene grew tense…

★ **Add an exciting ending to Lady Myrtle's story, using transitional expressions to make your paragraphs read more smoothly.**

Smooth Connections

In a relay race, a runner completes her section of the race and then hands the baton to the next runner. If something goes wrong in that exchange between the runners, the entire team can lose.

And so it goes with sentences. The writer needs to move smoothly from one sentence to the next and from one paragraph to the next. One way to do this is by using *transitions*. Transitions are words and phrases that connect the parts of a piece of writing. They relate one idea to a previously mentioned idea. Here are just a few common transitional expressions:

> although • after • afterward • also • and • before • besides
> but • eventually • finally • first • however • meanwhile • next
> similarly • since • then • today • unless • until • while

Without good transitions, a paragraph can sound rough and choppy, even robot-like. Here is an example of a paragraph without any transitions:

My trip with Aunt Zelda was more than I had bargained for. She said we would be flying. She didn't say that she would be the pilot. We departed on Monday morning just before dawn. We flew to Tennessee. We visited the Cave of the Woodchucks. We went to North Dakota to the barbed wire museum. We refueled in Bismarck. We took off for northern Idaho. We landed in a potato field. The farmer offered us potato root beer. We declined. Aunt Zelda said she was the designated flyer. She had to stay alert. We laughed. We flew off to Denver. We flew over Mile High Stadium. We accidentally became part of the aerial half-time show at a Broncos' game. We flew home. I never thought I would be glad to see Ohio.

Now here is an example of the same paragraph with transitions added:

*My trip with Aunt Zelda was more than I had bargained for. She said we would be flying, **but** she didn't say that she would be the pilot. We departed on Monday morning just before dawn **and** flew to Tennessee. We visited the Cave of the Woodchucks. **Then** we went to North Dakota to the barbed wire museum. We refueled in Bismarck **and** took off for northern Idaho. We landed in a potato field. The farmer offered us potato root beer, **but** we declined. Aunt Zelda said that **since** she was the designated flyer, she had to stay alert. We laughed **and** flew off to Denver. We flew over Mile High Stadium **and** accidentally became part of the aerial half-time show at a Broncos' game. **Finally,** we flew home. I never thought I would be glad to see Ohio.*

★ Rewrite the story below, putting in some transitional expressions like *first, then, next, after* and *finally*. (You may have to add or rearrange a few words to make the paragraph read as it should.)

I went into the kitchen, quietly. I opened the cupboard. I got out a mousetrap. I spread open the wire bar. I put in a piece of cucumber smeared with peanut butter. I set the trigger of the trap. I gently laid it on the shelf under the sink. I closed the cupboard door under the sink. The trap snapped shut. I was afraid to look under the sink. I went back to bed. I had nightmares about mouse homicide court.

Tied Up

Transitional devices tie sentences (and their ideas) together, making your writing read smoothly. One transitional device is the use of synonyms—words with the same meaning as words used earlier in your writing.

If you are writing about a dog your brother brought home, you might use some of the following synonyms for dog: *puppy, hound, mongrel, mutt, collie, beast, creature, canine, pooch, pup.* These key words, scattered throughout the paragraph, would help pull your message together. They would make the paragraph read more smoothly than it would if you kept repeating the word *dog*.

In the following paragraph, the author has helped tie the paragraph together by using synonyms for "black box":

> The citizens of Gwark had never seen such a thing—a black box with small turquoise levers on the sides. When the levers were depressed, the **instrument** gave out a mournful wail, like someone falling out of a hot-air balloon. The citizens were afraid of the **device** at first and used it only during war against the Zitboys, who lived in a lower galaxy. The Gwark King played the **machine** day and night: "Eeeeeeeeeeeeew, oooooooooooow, uuuuuuuuuuuuuuuuuuw," it moaned, scaring the Zitboys half to death. They were sure it was some new kind of torture **device.**
>
> Within three light-years the Zitboys surrendered to the Gwarks. The black box was placed on an altar in the Great Hall of Megon, and all the children of Gwark came daily to see the **contraption** that had made them rulers of the seventh universe.

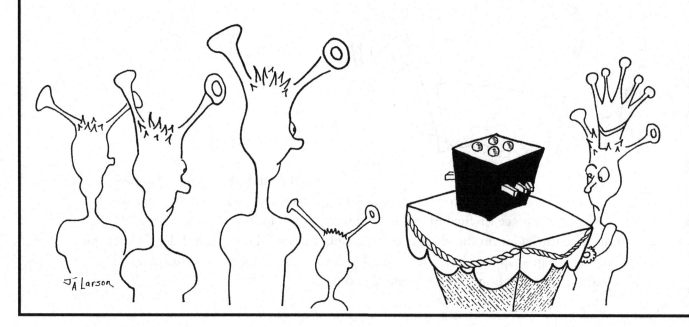

★ Imagine that someone has just discovered a strange, prehistoric creature. Write **10-15** sentences about the creature, using *synonyms* to make the sentences read smoothly. Tell how the creature was discovered, when it was discovered, where it was discovered, how old it is, how dangerous it is, what its habits and behaviors are and how useful it is to humans.

Remember: Do not repeat the word "creature" again and again in your paragraphs. Use synonyms like *animal, reptile, organism, living thing*, etc.

Draw a picture of the creature to go along with your description.

Connecting with Pronouns

Transitional devices help make a piece of writing read smoothly. One transitional device is the use of pronouns. Repeating the same word over and over again can make a paragraph sound choppy. Using pronouns like *it, he, she* or *they* can really help.

Here is an example of a paragraph without pronouns:

Kayla walked into the pet store with fifteen dollars. Kayla laid her money on the counter. Kayla said Kayla wanted 24 goldfish to feed Kayla's seal named Bob. The pet store owner, who loved goldfish, was disgusted. The pet store owner said that if Kayla wanted seal food Kayla could go find Mrs. Paul's fish sticks at the grocery store.

Obviously, there are too many "Kayla's" in this paragraph. Using the pronoun *she* makes the name Kayla less distracting and helps move the story along more smoothly.

*Kayla walked into the pet store with fifteen dollars. **She** laid her money on the counter. **She** said **she** wanted 24 goldfish to feed her seal named Bob. The pet store owner, who loved goldfish, was disgusted. **He** said that if Kayla wanted seal food **she** could go find Mrs. Paul's fish sticks at the grocery store.*

★ Make up a name for the person in the illustration. Tell what he is doing and what happens next. Try to use his name only once or twice. Use pronouns to make your writing read smoothly.

Three in One

Transitional devices help hold a piece of writing together. They help it read smoothly. Here are three common kinds of transitions:

---

1. Using **transitional expressions** (connecting words) like *first, then, next, afterward, finally, at last,* etc.

2. Using **synonyms** for key words, instead of repeating the same words over and over again.

3. Using **pronouns** like *he* or *she,* instead of repeating a name over and over again.

★ **Below is a story that uses the three transitional devices mentioned above. Circle all the transitions.**

Pecos Pete walked into the town of Tulip just before sundown. He set his laptop computer on the Tomb of the Unknown Grocer and said, "My machine can whip any dimwitted, hot-wired, battery-powered piece of electronics in this town."

First the people were frightened. Then one small lady from the U-Name It shop said, "My PeachPit 5000 will beat yours with three minutes to spare, or you can have every close-out coupon I've got in my purse."

Pecos Pete roared, "I'm the laptopping-est, smooth typing-est, rip-roarin' digital sound byting-est critter that ever typed a memo. You're on, Missy!"

The contest lasted two hours.

Finally, the mayor declared the competition closed. "The winner and computing champion is Ms. Mulldoop!"

Pecos Pete's new laptop computer was coughing and wheezing like a tired horse. He was sweating like a dishrag. "All right, lady, you win. But be prepared to lose next time. Then I'll bring my handbook along, and also a friend of mine from Texas who can read!"

★ Practice using transitions by writing a description of what is happening in the illustration below. Name the person and describe the events—not only what is happening at the moment but what will happen in the near future. Use three different kinds of transitions in your sentences to make the paragraph read smoothly.

In Focus

General statements are like photos out of focus. They are vague and uninteresting. It is a writer's job to paint clear word pictures with interesting details. Here is an example of a general statement:

The statue of Rosalie Popplenip sometimes looks somewhat scary.

Here is a more detailed version that brings the picture into focus.

When fading sunlight casts shadows across the sunken cheeks of Rosalie Popplenip, the statue of Gupperville's most famous undertaker, little children and adults race past with fear.

★ **The story below is full of vague, general statements. After reading through it once, rewrite the story, using descriptive details that will make it come sharply into focus. Remember that readers like to "see" what is going on. Use specific colors, shapes, movements, names, expressions, comments by characters and exciting action words to give your readers something clear to look at.**

A Story About a Girl

A girl had an active imagination. She always saw things that no one else saw. When she told other people about what she saw, they often laughed at her.

One day she overheard someone talking on the telephone. She jumped to the wrong conclusions about what she heard. She did something stupid. She learned an important lesson.

DownWrite Funny © Taylor & Francis   DOI: 10.4324/9781003234715-8

UnCool

Vague words like "cool" or "awesome" or "radical" don't really say much of anything. To one person, "cool" might describe someone who practically lives on a skateboard. To another, "cool" might describe someone smart enough to do all her math homework in her head.

Good writers use specific words that describe *exactly* what they mean.

★ **Rudolph may be the most famous reindeer of all, but Blitzen has been called the "coolest." Write a brief description of Blitzen, pictured above. How does the coolest of all Santa's reindeer actually live his deer life? You might want to describe Blitzen's clothes, his apartment, his snack food and his hobbies. Make your description create a clear picture.**

"Awesome" Isn't Good Enough

Suppose someone writes, "You should see Mollie Crater's pet orangutan. It is *awesome*!"

This description is vague because it uses the empty word "awesome." "Awesome" can mean almost anything you want it to mean. Is Mollie's orangutan awesome because it juggles avocados? Because it can outrun the postman? Because it smells like old gym socks? Because it's the color of creamed corn? A more effective description would tell exactly what is so "awesome" about the orangutan.

★ Take a minute to write some sentences about one of Mollie Crater's *other* pets. Avoid general words like *awesome, cool, excellent, weird* and *nice*. Give a clear picture of the animal. Tell the reader how the animal looks, acts, even smells. Use a thesaurus or dictionary to find adjectives and verbs to help the reader *see* what you are saying.

If you like, add a drawing of Mollie's pet. However, be sure that the words themselves create a vivid picture of the animal.

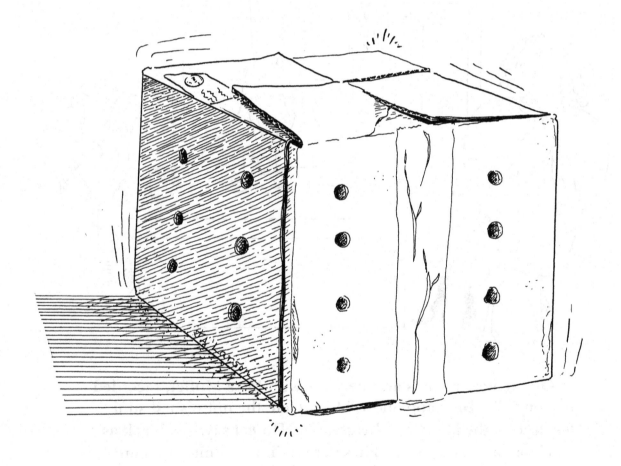

Simple Similes

Imagine that you are walking down Fifth Avenue and hear a strange sound. Later, when you try to describe the sound, you can't find the words to describe it exactly. What you need is a *simile*. With a simile, you can compare the strange sound to something more familiar. For example, you might say, "I heard a voice that sounded like a loon playing a bagpipe," or "The voice was as squeaky as the lid of a vampire's coffin." Comparisons like these, using the words "like" or "as," are called *similes*. Similes can be very useful in creating word pictures.

★ On the next page is an interview with Miss Muffet, recorded live on "The Bill Sapp Show." Complete the unfinished similes used in the interview. Be creative. Do *not* say: "as black as coal" or "as cold as ice." These are ordinary similes that are overused. Try something original.

DOI: 10.4324/9781003234715-9

Bill Sapp: You've never been on our show. Thanks for stopping by.

Miss Muffet: I'm as thrilled as _____to be here.

Bill Sapp: Well isn't that nice. Let's begin with what I'm sure is a difficult topic for you. Tell our audience how you became addicted to cheese.

Miss Muffet: I was young and as dumb as _____ when I first came to my grandparents' farm in upstate New York.

Bill Sapp: We know that. We all read the poem about you being terrified of a stupid spider.

Miss Muffet: That spider wasn't stupid. He was as smart as _____.

Bill Sapp: Well, fine. But what about your cheese addiction?

Miss Muffet: That came much later, on a night that was as dark as

_____.

Bill Sapp: Skip the weather reports. Have you beaten the addiction? Are you free from the power of cheese?

Miss Muffet: I was never addicted to cheese. It was the *whey* that I was so fond of. I enjoyed whey as much as a _____ enjoys _____.

Bill Sapp: Did the spider get you hooked? Is that why you were afraid of him?

Miss Muffet: I was NOT afraid of him. I was allergic. He crept up next to me as silently as _____, and I broke out in hives.

Bill Sapp: So you didn't leave your little sitting stool because you were frightened?

Miss Muffet: No. I'm not the kind of girl to be pushed off a stool. The hives made me as itchy as _____. I had to run or go mad.

Bill Sapp: You seem well now.

Miss Muffet: I'm as fit as a fiddle.

Bill Sapp: That's a rather weak simile for a girl as talented as you.

Miss Muffet: Okay. I'm as fit as _____.

Metaphorically Speaking

To make descriptions more direct and more powerful, writers often use a form of figurative language called *metaphor*. A metaphor compares two things that seem very different but are really similar in a deeper, more meaningful way. For example, if your grandmother calls you a "peach," she does not mean that you are yellow and hang from a fruit tree. She means that you are sweet, pleasant, enjoyable—like a peach.

Similarly, a computer might not seem at first to have much in common with a dinosaur. However, you might write a metaphor that says, "Roger's computer is a dinosaur, so old that there are no others like it left in the universe."

★ **The paragraph below is full of metaphors. Circle each metaphor that you find.**

I was at K-Mart when an announcer spoke over the intercom: "All customers please assemble in the center of the store. A tornado is approaching." Shopping quickly became a nightmare. I was a turtle scurrying for cover as I dipped under a table of mouthwash on sale for $1.29. I shivered and shook. My mouth was a dry dishcloth. My tongue was a Brillo pad. My toes were claws gipping the inside of my Himalayan hiking boots, on special for $31.95 if you bought two pair.

Suddenly the flashing blue light in the panty hose aisle fizzled. The store lights went black. The place became a tomb of silence. I thought of all the shopping I would never do, all the blue-light specials I would miss. Then the lights snapped on and the announcer said, "Sorry for the scare, folks. The tornado went south."

I danced. I sang. I was a ballerina in hiking boots. I had faced the monster and survived. I would live to shop another day.

★ The chubby monkey on the left is **Albert**. The only thing he loves more than junk food is **Madge**, the beautiful movie star, now retired, who is sitting next to him. In the picture below, the two monkeys are engaged in "love talk."

"Come and sit closer, my little **Pop Tart**," Albert croons.
"Not right now, you chocolate-frosted hunk of angel food cake," Madge replies.

Finish the monkeys' conversation, using six more junk food metaphors. In other words, write at least six complete sentences containing metaphors that have to do with food.

Word Magic

Writers are like magicians. They can create amazing illusions. Magicians use special equipment and tricks to create their illusions. Writers use only words—a few good *details* in the right place at the right time.

Imagine an empty street. A good writer might use words to create two entirely different impressions of that street. He might describe the street as if it is full of promise and possibility, or full of terror and uncertainty. Read the following descriptions of Maple Street, for example:

Maple Street #1—Maple Street lay bare in the early dawn, its cobbled bricks absorbing the warmth of the rising sun. Soon children would be running their bikes up and down the sidewalks, mothers would be pushing their infants in strollers toward the park, and business people would be opening their shops and setting out tables for early morning customers who like a good cup of coffee to start the day.

Maple Street #2—Maple Street was deserted as the wind whipped across its cold cobbled surface. Empty cans rattled over the bricks like clinking, hollow bells echoing loneliness and fear. There was no one, not a single soul, on the street or in the shops or even driving by. The street was like a graveyard with neat green grass and stiff benches where no one sat to pass the time of day.

In Maple Street #1, which details help create the image of a happy, pleasant place?

_____

_____

_____

_____

In Maple Street #2, which details help create the image of a cold, deserted place?

_____

_____

_____

DOI: 10.4324/9781003234715-10

★ Look closely at the illustration above. Then write two different descriptions of the scene—one that is positive (happy, hopeful, pleasant, encouraging) and one that is negative (gloomy, uncertain, even frightening). Choose your details carefully to create a specific mood.

Getting Rid of the Gray

What if everything you saw was gray—your skin, your hair, the sky, your food, your neighborhood, your pets, your parents, the ocean, trees, cars, books, fingernail polish and Big Macs? How exciting would life be?

Some people write "gray" stories and "gray" poems and "gray" news reports. They use lifeless, colorless words that make their writing dull and uninteresting. They leave out all the wonderful *details* worth noticing and writing about.

Here is an example of a gray, dull paragraph:

Dinner at my friend Tricia's house was rather unusual. I was quite disturbed with the way things worked. In fact, at one point I became a bit anxious and had to excuse myself from the table. When I came out of the bathroom her family was waiting for me with a strange dessert.

Here is the same paragraph with some life and color added:

I thought that my family was weird until I had dinner at my friend Tricia's house. Her father stood up and flipped a chicken wing onto each person's plate, using a miniature catapult that he had built out of chewed-on pencils. Then Tricia's mother poured frozen peas in the toaster and said, "It's like the Fourth of July when the toaster pops." Tricia's brother ate creamed corn and strawberry Twinkies while Tricia drank pink lemonade with sticks of broccoli in it. I excused myself and hid in the bathroom. When I came out, they were all waiting for me with a dessert—a big red bowl of baked tomatoes topped with chocolate chips and whipped cream. For the first time ever, I wished I could skip dessert.

★ **Read the gray, dull sentences in bold type, below. Rewrite each sentence, adding details that bring each one to life. Choose some of the questions in parentheses to help you.**

1. **Spring break was a positive experience.** (Did you travel far? Who went along? What did you do for fun? What food did you eat? Did you meet new people? What new sights did you see?)

2. **Nothing on the plate was like real food.** (What color was the food? What texture? What did it smell like? What shape was it? Was it cooked all the way through?)

3. **The party was boring.** (What kind of music was playing? How many kids were there? What kind of food was served? Where did the party take place?)

4. **Our house is a three-ring circus every morning.** (What does that mean? What happens?)

Face It

Glue Boy has struck again! After cementing 31 jumbo jets to the runway at Denver International Airport, Glue Boy flew to Europe and glued EuroDisney's Big Thunder Mountain roller coaster in a permanently upside down position.

You were there. You caught a glimpse of Glue Boy's fiendish, globetrotting face, and now you must describe to authorities what he looks like.

★ **Using the list of descriptive words below for help, write a complete description of Glue Boy, from the neck up. Be clear. Be specific. This glue-happy maniac must be stopped!**

Lips
rubbery
heart-shaped
loose
full
puckered
pursed
narrow
thin
thick
drooping
chapped
puffy
angelic
fleshy
curling

Nose
hooked
bulbous
flat
pointed
flared
pierced
bent
swollen
jutting

impish
mountainous
ruddy
dainty
crooked
blunt
lumpish
upturned
stubby
arched

Eyes
bloodshot
pale
pink
empty
sparkling
ocean blue
oil-black
nut-brown
lively
piercing
dark
dangerous
shining
diamond
almond

wide
staring
fishy
cow-like
deer-like
ancient
watery
bright
glassy
dreamy

Eyebrows
arched
drooping
heavy
hairless
thin
trimmed
bushy
tangled
thick
brooding

Ears
egg-shaped
dainty
sagging

elfish
bulging
pointed
jutting
tapering
Spock-like
bell-shaped
peaked
crinkly
notched
pierced
tiny
floppy
oval
round
symmetrical
misshapen
huge

Chin
jutting
square
fleshy
bony
crescent-shaped
pointy
dimpled

smooth
hairy
warty
scarred
wide
narrow
pink
double

Cheeks
doughy
chubby
pocked
freckled
wrinkled
puffy
rosy
pimply
dimpled
tattooed
angular
sunken
gaunt

Hair
shining
stringy
brown
blonde
brunette
red
black
straight
curly
wavy
bobbed
spiked
dry
permed
nonexistent
fly-away
thin

thick
wiry
soft
sweet-smelling
long
short
braided
in a pony tail
in pig tails
in dread locks
shaved

Neck
long
short
crooked
sunburned
graceful
stocky
nonexistent

Eyelashes
brown
fake
blonde
black
red
long
short
curled
straight
thick
thin

Jowls
droopy
hanging
wrinkled

Forehead
high
low

wrinkled
brooding
prominent
scarred
oily

Mouth
curled
red
small
large
grinning
smirking
wide
narrow
frowning
smiling

Teeth
pearly white
yellow
stained
buck
large
small
straight
crooked
gold
silver
false
with braces
sharp
jagged
broken
missing

Common Sense

There is one language in the world that all people share: the language of the senses. That's why good writers use words that appeal to the senses: *shrieked* (sound); *buttery* (taste); *prickly* (touch); *glowing* (sight); and *pungent* (smell).

★ **The box below contains a collection of sensory words. Make five columns on a sheet of paper, one for each of the five senses: s***ound, taste, touch, sight* **and** *smell.* **Then sort the words into categories. Put those that appeal to sight in the sight category, those that appeal to sound in the sound category, etc.**

There are at least 10 words for each column. Some columns may have as many as 28 words.

---

red • squawk • sour • smooth • acrid • short • hissing • salty
slimy • musty • unpainted • scream • scratchy • moldy • honk
toot • purr • sizzle • spicy • scaly • rank • tilted • moan
delicious • sticky • sulphurous • oval • croak • scrumptious
humid • pungent • skinny • yowl • screech • tweet • cheesy •
oily aromatic • pitted • lemony • peppery • whine • roar • bark
bleat • curved • straight • gray-haired • triangular • wavy
rounded • pointy • jingling • banging • snapping • crackling
popping • sweet • bitter • nutty • creamy • dusty • moist • icy
clammy • rotten • smokey • fragrant • soggy

★ Now, write a paragraph that tells what is going on in the illustration below. Use at least **10** sensory words in your description. Circle each sensory word that you use.

Virtual Reality

In this age of computers, people talk about "virtual reality," or creating what *almost* seems real. The human imagination is the best virtual reality machine in the universe. Good writers appeal to the imagination by using sensory words. Sensory words help readers create images in their minds that seem almost (or "virtually") real.

For example, instead of writing, ***Jeremy is such a pig when it comes to movie popcorn,*** a good writer helps the reader create a much more vivid picture, using sensory words: ***Jeremy buried his head in the extra-large bag of popcorn until he had slurped and snorted and chomped every last kernel. For the rest of the movie, he had a greasy film around his mouth, and he smelled like butter.***

★ Imagine yourself in one of the situations below. Write a short paragraph describing your experience. What information would your senses pick up? Tell what you might see, smell, hear, taste and touch. Be brief. Be accurate. Give your readers a sense of "virtual reality."

- **Situation #1**—You have been accidentally locked in a mall and have no money for the pay phone. You will have to spend the night. What might you hear? See? Smell? Taste? Touch?

- **Situation #2**—Your spaceship has left you on the surface of the moon while it heads back to the space station to pick up more dried ice cream. What will you touch, taste, smell, hear and see while you're wandering around on your own?

Reminder:

Sensory words are words that help readers see, hear, smell, touch or taste in their imaginations. If you are reading about a hospital emergency room and start feeling slightly ill, the writer has probably used a lot of sensory words.

★ Describe what is happening in the picture below, using as many sensory words as possible.

Generic Images

A generic image is like a generic cereal box. It is black and white, ordinary and plain. Take a look at this generic sentence:

A strange parade went past my front porch last Saturday.

A more interesting, colorful description uses sensory words—words that appeal to the five senses:

I was sitting on my front porch last Saturday when a flatbed truck rolled by, carrying six women in yellow goggles. Their black snorkels blew green iridescent bubbles into the afternoon light as the truck belched fumes that smelled like burnt rubber. The only sound was the crunch of the leaves under the feet of a marching band of kazoo players. The kazoo players remained silent. So did the clown riding in the convertible behind them and tossing hard-boiled eggs at people passing by…

★ **Read the generic sentences below. Rewrite each one, adding color, size, texture, sound, shape, taste, smell—whatever sensory words you can use that will fill the image with life and feeling.**

1. The woman was short and poorly dressed; she pushed a grocery cart wherever she went.

_____

_____

_____

2. The library was not very up-to-date.

_____

_____

_____

3. The ice cream cone was made of three scoops, which were rapidly melting.

_____

_____

_____

4. The empty subway was full of spray-painted messages and bad smells.

_____

_____

_____

5. Broken pieces of athletic equipment littered the locker room.

_____

_____

★ **Use colorful words to describe, with feeling, what the man in the picture might see, smell, hear, taste and touch.**

Details for Atmosphere

Places have **atmosphere.** Atmosphere has to do with the overall mood or feeling of a place.

A dimly lit restaurant might have a romantic atmosphere, for example. Or it might have a tacky, run-down feeling about it. An empty lot might feel dangerous, or it might have a playful, friendly atmosphere.

Suppose that you want to describe a teenager's room that is crammed full of stuff. You certainly don't want to describe every single thing. To give the reader an accurate impression of the room without listing everything in it, you might select just a few revealing details that capture the mood of the room.

For example, mentioning the brightly colored, silly items like stuffed dinosaurs or plastic tulips could help create a light-hearted, happy atmosphere. Mentioning the spider web and the horror movie poster might help create a dark or even dangerous atmosphere.

The words you choose to describe these items are also important. "There is a creepy poster on the wall" doesn't do much to create a mood. "Blood drips from a hairy claw in the poster on the wall" does more to establish a dark mood.

★ **On the next page is a long list of items sometimes found in teenagers' rooms. Choose 10 items and include them in a description of an imaginary room. Create a clear atmosphere or mood with your description.**

Then choose 10 *different* items and describe a different room, this time creating a *different* mood or atmosphere.

Here are some ideas for the atmospheres or moods you might want to create:

Happy	**Childish**
Hi-tech	**Frilly**
Studious	**Macho**
Gloomy	**Cold and unfriendly**
Whimsical or silly	**Warm and friendly**
Sophisticated	**Dreamy**
Athletic	**Practical**
Sloppy	

Items: loafers • ballet shoes • work boots • combat boots • basketball shoes • nylon stockings • sweat socks • white anklets • baseball cards • soccer shorts • tennis balls • squid aquarium • used cereal boxes • ripped T-shirts • whale posters • soccer ball • aluminum pop-top chain • encyclopedias • dictionaries • super hero comic books • Garfield cartoon books • San Diego Chargers bedspread • poster of silver skull • 56 romance novels • basketball hoop • CDs • DVDs • iPod • uneaten burrito • squirt guns • hair curlers • a life-sized poster of Brad Pitt • computer • mini-television • head phones • colored pencils • rollerblades • sleeping bag • basket of wrinkled sweatshirts • pink curtains • Winnie the Pooh diary • trumpet • guitar • flute • tuba • hair dryer • kitty cat clock • waterbed • photos from Camp Ringworm • copies of *Seventeen* magazine • snowshoes • black leather gloves • boxing gloves • silk dress • black leather jacket • mobile made of used motorcycle parts • whitewashed dresser • two first-place blue ribbons • teddy bears • 3' tall stuffed gorilla • life-sized poster of LeBron James • Hello Kitty pillow • Superman underwear • broken football helmet • blush • 57 mystery novels • basket of assorted eye shadows • copy of the *Wall Street Journal* • two novels by Stephen King • aerial maps of Cleveland, Ohio • makeup brushes • green rubber ducky • cat toys • live rabbit in a cage • bean bag chair • tennis racket and balls • picture of Grandma • movie ticket stubs • concert ticket stubs • framed perfect attendance certificate • music box with a pop-up ballerina • 15 pairs of earrings • dried-up corsage from the Christmas dance • painting of the human brain • 4' tall lava lamp • collection of stuffed bears • trophy • six brushes • 12 combs • 41 used towels • live tarantula in a cage • oak book shelf • red accordion with the name "Kelly" on it in rhinestones • gray metal dresser • grow light for ferns • camera • digital camera • archery target • vase • hat rack • dart board • fishing pole • skate board • volleyball shoes • 12 empty oatmeal boxes • four necklaces • fluffy white robe • rolling pin • pet rat • deck of cards • shaving cream

Focal Points

When describing an object, it's best to start at a **focal point** and move logically from top to bottom, from bottom to top, from left to right, from front to back or in some other order.

For example, if you want to describe the world's ugliest insect, you might start by describing the face, then the body, then the feet, as in the example below:

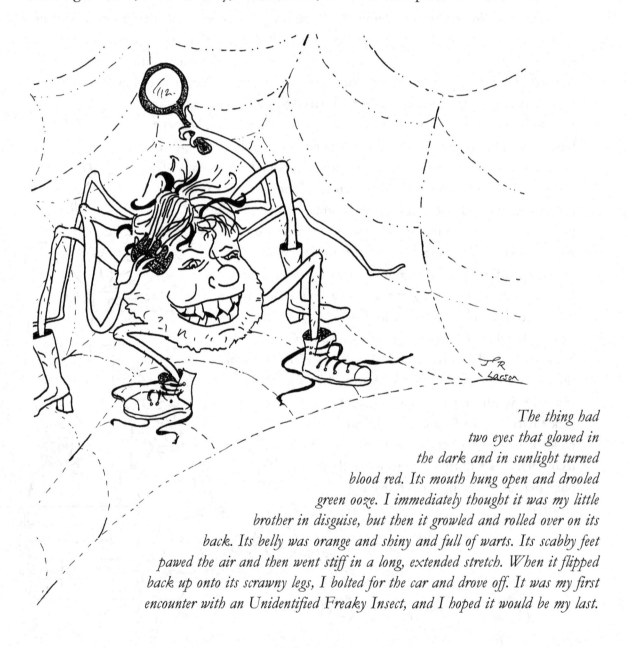

The thing had two eyes that glowed in the dark and in sunlight turned blood red. Its mouth hung open and drooled green ooze. I immediately thought it was my little brother in disguise, but then it growled and rolled over on its back. Its belly was orange and shiny and full of warts. Its scabby feet pawed the air and then went stiff in a long, extended stretch. When it flipped back up onto its scrawny legs, I bolted for the car and drove off. It was my first encounter with an Unidentified Freaky Insect, and I hoped it would be my last.

DOI: 10.4324/9781003234715-13

★ Draw a picture of your own **UFI** (Unidentified Freaky Insect). Then describe the creature you have drawn, starting from a single focal point and moving logically along, left to right, top to bottom, back to front or in some other order.

Focus Attention

When writing a description, it is important to use details. However, it is also important to choose the details carefully and to organize them so that they make sense. If you include lots of boring details in a haphazard way, you will lose your reader.

To decide what details to include, choose a focal point. What is most important about the scene you are describing? What should be the focus? Begin your description at the focal point and then move logically along, from top to bottom, left to right, front to back or in some other logical pattern.

For example, to describe the picture below, you might begin with the Thing's eyes, since it is looking at itself in the mirror. After describing the eyes, you might move on down to the mouth and neck, to the arms and finally to the three feet with their long toenails. You would probably ignore details about the tree stump the Thing is sitting on or the shelf the mirror is resting upon. Describing these items would just take attention away from the really important part of the picture: the Thing.

★ Choose one of the "Things" listed below, and draw a picture of it. Then write a brief description of the Thing, beginning at a focal point and moving along in a logical pattern.

- An atomic-powered meatloaf maker
- An undersea creature
- A new species of hall monitor
- A beast in your neighbor's basement
- The unearthed remains of a prehistoric math teacher
- The sandwich in your little brother's backpack
- Professor Tweet's homemade alarm clock
- A statue honoring cranky librarians
- Myrna Swart's birthday cake
- Uncle Fred's dog, Bobo
- A high-tech eyebrow plucker
- A board game called "Knitting Dangerously"
- The all-new "Robo-Teacher"
- A three-eyed baby frog who was born next to the local nuclear power plant
- A vicious pet rock
- The newest laser mouse trap

Step by Step

In describing things, it's usually a good idea to have a plan. You might start at the left and move to the right in describing your subject. Or you might start at the top and move down.

Some objects lend themselves to different descriptive plans. Take, for example, our galaxy. There is no "left" or "right" or "up "or "down" in the universe. Out there in the black beyond, it might be better to use "inward toward the center" or "outward from the center."

A city could be described in the same way:

From a distance the city looked like a string of lights coiled and tangled upon itself, with the brightest lights burning in the center. But as we came closer, the scattered remains of junkyards and steel mills and factories filled the horizon. We drove through a maze of homes lining the concrete streets, then rows of shops and shopping malls. Finally the towers rose before us, like rockets aimed at the sky, and we knew we were at the center of the city.

Reminder:

Here are some good words to use in describing something logically: *first, then, next, farther on, after that, finally,* etc. Use these to move your reader along in your writing.

★ For years students have wondered what lies at the center of Ms. Huff's giant beehive hairdo. The only student who ever tried to find out disappeared ten years ago. What do you think is lurking under Ms. Huff's hairdo? A rubber chicken? A lamp? A real beehive?

Write a description of Ms. Huff's ancient hairdo, beginning with the outside layers and working in toward the center. Use vivid details to make your description lively and interesting.

Too Much of a Good Thing

A few well-chosen details make a piece of writing interesting and help communicate your message. However, it is possible to have too much of a good thing. You don't want to include so many details that you put your readers to sleep or confuse them with too much information.

You also don't want to repeat yourself. Too many words clutter your message. For example, there is no reason to say, "We had this huge, giant pizza after the game." The words *huge* and *giant* mean the same thing. It's better to use only one of them.

★ **The three paragraphs in the following story are cluttered with extra words. As you read, cross out each extra word that you find. Look for double describers like "old, ancient," "bright, shiny," "used, worn," etc.**

Trek to Mount Oregano

The tired weary group continued trudging and marching through the dense thick jungle,

looking for the lost city of Pasta. It was getting dark. As Pamela climbed Mount Oregano,

she could hear far-off distant drums. The sound sent chills up her spine. She shiv-

ered and said, "Rupert, bring me the big giant

squirt gun."

The path was so overgrown that Pamela

couldn't see anything ahead of her. She loaded

the squirt gun with diet sugar-free soda and

squeezed the trigger. Immediately the green

leaves on the bushes turned brown and fell off.

Reminder:

Keep your details under control. Don't describe every hair on the family cat, for example. Just focus on the ones that fell out on the counter and wound up in the split pea soup. It is important to be selective.

DownWrite Funny © Taylor & Francis

DOI: 10.4324/9781003234715-14

The path cleared. Pamela and her troupe proceeded until they came to an ancient old shrine. It was an important special moment. The group was getting nearer and closer to the lost city.

"We must go on," Pamela urged. Suddenly, there was a shout…

★ **When you finish circling all the wasted words, continue the story of Pamela's adventure, carefully avoiding extra words and unnecessary details.**

Description Out of Whack

Details are very important in good writing, but it is easy to overdo it. Overdone, unnecessary description is distracting to readers.

For example, imagine receiving a party invitation like this:

You are invited to a party at 1320 Martinez Place at 7:00 PM. *Please come in the back door. There's a good sidewalk back there made of lovely blue-gray stones taken from the cold, clear waters of Platypus Creek.*

Who cares about the lovely blue-gray stones? The important things to know are the time and location of the party. The other details are silly and annoying, wasting words and the reader's time.

However, in a different situation those stones might be important. Suppose that a newspaper reporter is doing a feature on the landscaping at 1320 Martinez Place. Then it might be quite appropriate to write about the sidewalk made of "lovely blue-gray stones taken from the cold, clear waters of Platypus Creek."

Reminder:

Don't write every single thought that comes into your head. Nobody is interested. Instead, choose your details carefully. Make sure you include only information that contributes to your story.

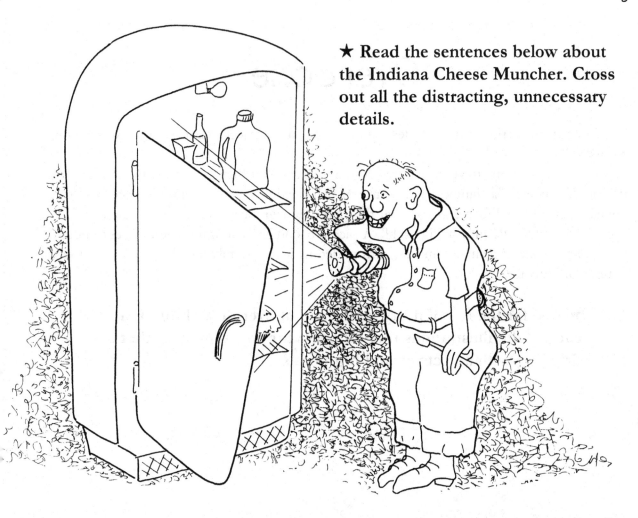

★ **Read the sentences below about the Indiana Cheese Muncher. Cross out all the distracting, unnecessary details.**

He slipped into the dark kitchen on a moonlit summer night and tip-toed up to the refrigerator in his new African hunting shoes that were as brown as fawn skin with bright green laces that looked like they had been dyed using real lime peels. The Cheese Muncher gently pulled open the door, which was as white as ice cream, smooth and shiny, with that just-wiped look of a door that is ready to get its picture taken. The light inside the fridge was out, so the Cheese Muncher flicked on his multi-use underwater galactic flashlight that was made by artistically challenged people in Seattle, a lovely place to visit in summer if you like to watch whales in the harbor spouting silver cascades of water.

★ **Now use your imagination and clear, descriptive words to complete the story. Choose only details that contribute to your story.**

Overdone

You can get carried away with description—too many adjectives, too many exclamation points!!!!!!!!

For example, some travel brochures describe places as if they are almost magical. A fish pond becomes "a shimmering expanse of fish-filled waters!" A train ride becomes "the travelling event of a lifetime as you soar through the magnificent wilderness in the comfort of your own elegantly furnished coach!" A picnic becomes "a stunning family event under the cooling shade of giant sycamores, surrounded by loving family members and sixty-four pounds of bratwurst!"

★ **Just for the fun of it, try your hand at over-describing. For each of the illustrations that follow, write two sentences that are dripping with adjectives and high praise.**

#1

#2

_____

_____

_____

_____

_____

_____

_____

#3

_____

_____

_____

_____

_____

_____

_____

_____

Plain Silly

Filling your writing with big words is like filling up a balloon too much—the whole thing blows up in your face. It's not that a big word is necessarily bad. Sometimes a big word is the only word that will do. However, too many big, "overblown" words make your writing silly and hard to understand. They may even make it hard for your reader to understand your meaning.

Look at the following sentence, for example: *Milly decided to prevaricate when her mother asked about the stained antimacassar.* It sounds as though someone is speaking with a mouthful of marbles. The sentence is much more effective like this: *Milly lied when her mother asked about the stained chair cover.*

Sometimes people get to thinking that they need to be brilliant in order to write. If they can't actually *be* brilliant, they figure they can at least *sound* brilliant. Instead of saying something simple like, "I love you," they say, "I am experiencing some profound emotional affection for you." Of course, the overblown words just confuse the message. Worse, they sound silly and insincere.

★ **Rewrite each sentence below into a simple statement. Make the meaning clear. You may need a dictionary to decode some of the long-winded words.**

1. She castigated him for gesticulating like a monkey when he talked.

_____

_____

2. Prevarication is a practice worth eschewing on a permanent basis.

_____

_____

3. Nothing can cause more consternation than a gravid elephant at a party.

_____

_____

4. The elves toiled for a fortnight without remuneration.

_____

5. Viola trapped the yegg in her bathroom and promptly excoriated him.

_____

_____

6. Pecos Sal's enervated palfrey would ambulate no farther.

_____

_____

★ Pretend you are running for District 4 Galaxy Council Representative. Both Earth and the planet Nitt-Witt are in your district. Since Nitt-Witt is crawling with creatures who understand only complicated, puffed-up, overblown words, you need to write two election speeches, one for Earth (where humans like plain, simple language) and one for Nitt-Witt (where the citizens like just the opposite).

First write your speech for Earthlings, telling why everyone should vote for you.

Then write your speech for Nitt-Wittians. Use your trusty intergalactic thesaurus to turn simple, direct words into long, overblown words that the Nitt-Wittians will understand.

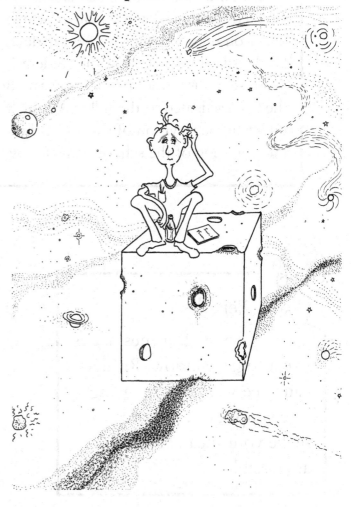

Big Words—Little Meaning

Big, clumsy words can ruin your writing. Don't say *countenance* when you can say *face*. Don't use the word *malevolent* when *evil* will do the job. In most cases, simple words communicate more clearly.

Vice Principal McFigit didn't communicate clearly when he wrote a discipline report on the two students in the illustration on the next page. His report is in the box below.

Swellville Middle School Discipline Report

FROM: Mr. McFigit
Re: Offense

On April 24, Mindy Wortt and Sammy Yunkova, both eighth graders, violated school ordinance #4025, which decrees that no osculation shall occur on school grounds. These malefactors engaged in this illicit activity on Wednesday at 10:00 AM in the student lounge area. Unless these perpetrators promise to display a more appropriate demeanor in the future, I recommend they be castigated to the full extent including detainment after regular hours under the supervision of Coach Michowski and being required to facilitate the sanitizing of the school premises by removing debris.

Reminder:

An unclear message is like a foggy window. Readers can't see what you're saying. Use simple, direct words to make your meaning as clear as possible.

★ Vice Principal McFigit wants his report published in the *Swellville Middle School Review.* You, the *Swellville Review's* editor, know that no one will understand the report unless you rewrite it.

Use a thesaurus and a dictionary, if necessary, to decode Mr. McFigit's complicated, overblown message. Use simple, clear words in your "translation."

It All Depends

Have you ever heard two different people tell two different stories about the same event? Sometimes the two versions bear very little resemblance to each other. That's because each person views the event from a different **perspective.**

A writer's perspective is his point of view. It is determined by such things as his age, experience, knowledge, culture, family, career, interests and upbringing. How each of us sees things depends a lot on where we have been and the kind of person we have become.

★ **Four people observed a fight break out in a school hallway. Each person wrote a brief description of what happened, from his or her perspective. Below is the first part of each description. Describe who might have written each report.**

_____ "Even though Brian has been warned about fighting, he still threw the first punch. He knows that is against school policy. We can't have students fighting in the hallway."

_____ "Brian hit Pete first, but Pete deserved it. He is such a jerk. He said something insulting about me, and Brian had to hit him."

_____ "I don't know who the two guys were, but they sure didn't know how to fight. I was cracking up just watching them."

_____ "I saw the two start to throw punches, and I was yelling like crazy for them to stop. I was afraid one of them was going to knock over that trash can I'd just filled with Styrofoam peanuts from some supplies we just got in. I sure didn't want to have to sweep up all those peanuts."

Reminder:

A perspective is neither right nor wrong. It just _is_. How we see something depends a lot upon where we are standing.

DOI: 10.4324/9781003234715-16

★ Four different people have walked past the scene illustrated below. Write a brief description of the event from the perspective of each individual. Write in the *first person*. In other words, use the word "I" and write as if the individual is telling the story himself or herself.

- a seven-year-old who lives on a farm
- a talent scout for the circus
- a fourteen-year-old girl who has seen it all
- an off-duty detective

Who's Talking?

The content of a story depends a lot upon who is telling it. If your brother tells about a disturbance at a rock concert, his version of what went on may be very different from the version told by the guards at the concert.

Both your brother and the guards would probably tell the story in the *first person*. That means that they would use the word "I" and tell about what happened from their own perspective.

A newspaper reporter, however, would probably write in the *third person*. She would not use the word "I" because she wouldn't be writing about what happened from her own personal point of view. She would be writing as an observer, just reporting the facts. She would use the pronouns *they, he* and *she* in telling the story.

Here is an example of a description written in the **first person:**

> *I'm not surprised I panicked when the submarine began its slow descent into the ocean. I don't even know why I got on that stupid thing in the first place. I hate small places. And I really hate being closed inside them with 29 other people. The place was so small even my big toe felt cramped. I also hate the dark. I can't believe they call those dinky little bulbs "lights." I've seen firefly runts brighter than those things.*
>
> *They turned on some sort of evil, rumbling generator that reminded me of Darth Vader's breathing. Then came the jolt. I don't know what it was, probably an overambitious great white whale. It knocked us all to one side of the vessel. That is when I fainted.*

Now read a description of the same event, this time written in **third person:**

> *The submarine sank slowly into the ocean until not a trace could be seen of it from the surface. A hush descended on all 30 people crowded aboard. Tiny bulbs threw eerie shadows across their faces. Several looked startled when the generator clicked on and started to hum loudly.*
>
> *Suddenly, the sub rolled over on its side, the result of a clumsy encounter with a coral reef. The passengers slid like smothered tamales to one side of the vessel. Before she hit the wall, one young woman turned a pale shade of green. Her eyes rolled upward, and she passed out cold just as a siren began blaring. Two men splashed bottled water on the young woman's face. Then they, too, started looking a little sick. One of the crew members wisely slid an empty wastepaper basket towards them and looked the other way.*

★ Write a paragraph based on the illustration below. Write about it from the perspective of the boy in the picture, in the first person. In other words, write as if the boy himself is telling the story. Use this opening line: *I woke up, hardly able to breathe. The sun was coming up, so I knew it was early. I tried to roll over but...*

★ Now write another paragraph based on the same illustration. This time write it in the third person. In other words, use the pronouns "they," "he" and "she" instead of the pronoun "I." Use this opening line: *Henry lay there like a hunk of cheese, squashed under the weight of his snoring pet pig.*

Description in Motion

You can't draw a picture of a thing called *joy*. You can't take a photograph of *worry* or *ambition*. These words express abstract ideas, ideas that you can't see or touch or grab hold of. To suggest ideas like these, writers often use actions or motions.

Think about a time when someone around you was happy. The person probably didn't walk right up to you and say, "You know what? I'm really happy. I'm *very* happy. Did you know I was happy?" You knew she was happy by reading the clues of her behavior. Maybe she was smiling. Or maybe she was laughing. It was her physical movements that made you see the joy she felt inside. In the same way, the best writers show how characters are feeling by showing their actions.

To show joy, a writer might have a character smile and laugh or walk with a bounce to her step. To show worry, a writer might describe a character frowning or pacing. To show ambition, a writer might describe a character working late into the night to study for a new job.

Suppose you are writing about Fred, an alien from another planet, and you want your readers to know about his fear of vegetables. You could say, **Fred, the alien, was terrified of vegetables.** That doesn't paint a very clear picture because there isn't any action. To paint a clearer picture of his fear, you might add some action to the description, like this: **Fred, the alien, ran from his space ship screaming, "It's carrots, I tell you! I can smell their orangey sweetness. Run for your lives! Hurry, or we'll all be killed!"**

Reminder:

Writing about what the character *does* is an effective way to show how he is feeling. If a character is depressed, the writer might describe him sitting in a darkened room staring at a humidifier. If a character is anxious, the writer might show him chewing the heads off of rubber darts as he paces in the driveway. Actions help illustrate feelings.

DOI: 10.4324/9781003234715-17

★ Angela is entering the classroom as a new student. Write a short paragraph or two showing what she is feeling, but without saying it outright. Instead, let her actions speak for themselves.

Think about these questions: Is Angela worried? Nervous? Terrified? Brave? Calm? Proud? Shy? Outspoken? How do you know? What does she do? What do others do? How does she react? What does she say?

Keep It Moving

Readers like to "see" what is going on when they read. A sentence like this doesn't help them see much:

There was an accident.

Most readers prefer words that help them picture what is going on:

An explosion ripped open the dairy, spewing milk into the air and raining cubes of butter onto the surrounding homes.

Action words help readers create pictures in their minds. Action words are words like "ripped" and "spewing" and "raining."

Here is another sentence that shows little action:

Jeanette saved the day by using duct tape on the lid of the cooler.

Here is how the sentence might read with some action words added:

*As a brown, shriveled claw **slid** out from under the lid of the cooler, Jeanette **sprang** for the duct tape, **ripped** off three silver strips and **stuck** the lid down before anyone in the library noticed.*

★ **Rewrite each of the following sentences so that they include vivid action words. Make sure your sentences help readers *see* what is going on.**

1. The baby ate the food.

   _____

   _____

2. Clarissa's mother had a fit when Clarissa came home late.

   _____

   _____

3. Bob arrived at home plate and scored a run.

   _____

   _____

4. The students were bored.

   _____

   _____

★ Describe what is happening in the scene below. If you like, use some of the action words in the box to help you with your description.

flipped • flopped • tossed • dumped • threw • aimed • caught • splattered
smashed • crunched • bashed • bonked • slipped • dodged • fell • dropped
whizzed • flew • shot • cruised • swung • swatted • smacked • plopped
tripped • leaped • screeched • seized • sprinted • skimmed • staggered
waddled • huddled • gulped • hunched • babbled • hollered • jerked • howled
marched • tackled • spiked • vaulted • dissected • wrestled • crammed
hopped • kissed • toppled • dipped • swirled • hauled • clipped • plastered
plowed • scraped • wiggled • scooped • scattered • piled • skinned • peeked
snickered • smudged • filtered • traced • tracked • sank • whined • worried
whispered • calculated • tugged • twinkled • locked • scrambled • fried

Cause and Effect

Most actions have an effect. That effect may cause another action, which causes another effect, which causes another action, and so forth. Here's an example:

> *A gentleman bends over to pick up a penny in a shopping mall, and his pants rip wide open. A kindergartner sees his flowered underwear, giggles and turns to tell her mother, who drops a jar of sauerkraut out of her grocery bag onto the floor. The jar breaks and the smell rushes out, drawing the attention of a teenager's pet iguana, which rushes over to investigate, pulling its master behind and causing...*

You get the idea. Sometimes this writing technique is called "cause and effect." When you show a reader what happens, you may also want to show what happens next.

★ **Use "cause and effect" to finish the description of the Pet Palace disaster illustrated on the next page. Describe what happens, one action at a time. Tell the effect of each action.**

Beware of using too many connecting words like *then, and so, next,* etc. Keep your sentences fairly short. Try to make your story ridiculous, with one bizarre event causing another even more bizarre event, and then another.

One more requirement: No "blood and guts," please.

Reminder:

Effects should be caused by something obvious to the reader. Don't write, "John entered the room and died." It is not clear how entering the room caused John's death. More information is needed. You might instead write, "John entered the room and stepped on a loose floor board. He lost his balance and hit his head, causing a brain injury that killed him only seconds later."

While his mother was buying fish food at the Pet Palace, Little Hal went around the store opening cages…

Answer Keys

Answer Key
Fragment Frustration, page 8

1. After the balloon toss, we took a break from playing games and ate pizza.
2. When the coyote king died, his subjects mourned the loss of their fearless leader.
3. When I came upon the scene, she was in shock and staring in disbelief.
4. By the time it was over, I was exhausted.
5. Her face breaks out in a rash when she eats pizza.
6. When the medicine kicked in, the old man felt so revived that he stood up and did a jig.
7. Along about midnight, the wolves began to howl from craggy perches in the foothills.
8. We found ticket stubs and loose change near the exit.
9. Next to her brother Jake loomed a menacing figure in the dark.
10. The rumors of a monster at the lake started because of the principal's cat.
11. Because of everything she had done for the past 16 years, her brother didn't want anything more to do with her.
12. Beneath the muddy water of Silver Lake near the town of Hackensack where my mother and her ex-husband live swims a monster with green eyes and a fierce growl.

<u>Beneath the muddy water of Silver Lake near the town of Hackensack where my mother and her ex-husband live</u> swims a monster with green eyes and a fierce growl—or so it is rumored.

One night along the shores of Silver Lake, the Hackensackians held a summer fair. I went with my friend Lisa and her younger brother Jake. We rode the Ferris wheel and participated in a balloon toss. <u>After the balloon toss,</u> we took a break from playing games and ate pizza. Lisa was reluctant to eat hers because sometimes her face breaks out in a rash <u>when she eats pizza.</u> Sure enough, it did that night, and she ran out of the fair to avoid people's stares.

We found ticket stubs and loose change <u>near the exit,</u> but no Lisa. As Jake and I realized that she was alone along the shores of Silver Lake, an image of a green-eyed growling monster came into my mind. Although I tried not to believe in monsters, I was worried about Lisa's safety.

Jake and I split up to look for her. After a while, I heard Lisa's cry in the distance. I ran toward the sound of her voice. <u>When I came upon the scene,</u> she was in shock and staring in disbelief. <u>Next to her brother Jake</u> loomed a menacing figure in the dark. It was the monster with two green, glowing eyes. We stood frozen, watching the creature until, finally, the two green eyes moved toward us.

"Maude!" we all exclaimed. The eyes, reflecting the moonlight and looking green, belonged to the principal's cat, Maude. As she crept out from beneath a shrub, we all laughed. The rumors of a monster at the lake had started <u>because of the principal's cat.</u> Maude had used the lake shores as her hunting grounds for years.

I picked Maude up and said, as we headed toward home, "No more hunting or haunting tonight, Maude. I'm through with this adventure." <u>By the time it was over,</u> I was exhausted.

Answer Key
Complete Thoughts, page 10

Today an accident occurred on County Road 34 involving a tricycle, a snake and a mystery cow. Nelda Niddlemeyer was pedaling her way down the road when she fell off her bike. She said she heard a loud "Pop!" and then she and the bike fell to the ground. "It was a back tire," she reported. She had just stopped off at Greasin' Gary's Garage to put air in all the tires. "**Because it was inflated** too much, the tire must have snagged on something and exploded."

When asked what she thought could have snagged her tire, she said, "I saw a snake in the road ahead of me. I kept riding and noticed the snake was headed for me, too. He didn't give me any initial trouble, but it was **after the snake slid by** that my tire popped. I think he may have bit my tire."

When she fell, Niddlemeyer said, she missed hitting a large Black Angus **by the skin of her teeth.** "The cow just appeared out of nowhere and spoke to me. I really felt like I was **in the danger zone** of the animal world."

When asked what the cow said, Niddlemeyer reported, "'Stop eating cows' or maybe it was 'stop eating.'"

Niddlemeyer, who was not hurt in the accident, has decided to change her life.

"I'm convinced that the snake and the cow were in cahoots. The snake made me fall, and then the cow verbally attacked me," Niddlemeyer decided. "From now on I won't order anything **other than french fries** at McDonalds. I don't need any more trouble from the League of Vegetarian Animals."

1. Boris Bleaker asked the stagecoach driver to stop when he recognized Punch Puttski, one of the boxing bunnies at the side of the road.
2. You can visit Aunt Rootie during the Christmas holidays but not without fruitcake from Schmitt's bakery as a gift.
3. During a blizzard, Snort Fordley enjoys riding around in his tow truck, looking for cars that are stuck in the ditch.
4. When Jerome spent $50 on fireworks for the 4th of July celebration, his sister thought he was completely insane.
5. Minnie Little Giraffe had to look for short trees to munch on because she was only seven feet tall.
6. Zelda Zitsfingle, a confirmed vegetarian, was totally disappointed when she hit the buffet line and saw there was nothing left to eat other than beef sandwiches.
7. Since he was kind of sloppy with an ink pen, George was glad he wasn't born before they invented pencils.
8. Lovely Princess Penelope sat on a hilltop in the golden mist of sunset and cried for her lost love.

Answer Key
No Jamming, page 12

On Goldfish Pond

Little Elsie was feeding the two-foot long white goldfish in the pond at the Castle Hotel. Her family stayed there every time her father went to the annual Disgruntled Postal Workers Convention in Iowa. Elsie liked the hotel because of the big fish under the fake drawbridge that led to the fake castle where all the guests slept.

As Elsie was feeding the big goldfish pieces of a sweet roll from the free continental breakfast by the fake swimming pool, she was startled by a tall man dressed like a knight and his red-haired friend, who were both carrying luggage for people out to their cars. She accidentally dropped the whole sweet roll into the pond, and the goldfish churned up the water trying to get at it. One elderly lady got scared and ran into the castle screaming, "Sharks! Sharks!" The manager raced outside to see what she was talking about and somehow knocked the redhead into the water. The redhead started yelling, "I'm allergic to fish. They'll kill me! They'll kill me!"

A guest on the fourth floor heard the screaming and tossed out ten bed sheets tied together to make a rope. He yelled, "Hang on!" The redhead hung on and was pulled 30 feet into the air, but just as he was about to be pulled to safety through the window, the sheets ripped. He fell like a stone on top of the knight, who was carrying duffel bags for sixteen fishermen in town for a carp derby. The knight toppled into the pond, almost drowning the elderly lady. She had come back outside, slipped on a stray piece of sweet roll and fallen into the pond. She was now treading water and screaming at the redhead. It was lucky that the knight had air bag underwear because the underwear blew up upon collision with the pond. The woman, the redhead and the knight were all three able to drift six feet to "shore," where the visiting fishermen were standing. One turned to the crowd and said, "Get me the net, boys. One of those is a keeper!"

After the fishermen rescued the three, everything seemed all right. The problems, however, were not over yet. After about five minutes in the sun, the soaking wet knight and all his armor turned into a big rusty tin can. He was frozen in one position until Otto, the mechanic, came with his trusty electric screwdriver to take the armor apart. This action proved to be even more embarrassing for the knight. Because his air bag underwear had exploded, he now had nothing on under his armor.

Then it turned out that the redheaded bell hop was not a redhead after all. As he floated in the pond, the dye from his hair started bleeding into the water, turning the pond water a bright red. The fish became sick from the dye, and a fish doctor had to be flown in from Timbuktu to care for them.

Finally, the elderly lady lost her favorite necklace on the nets that were used to rescue her. One of the older, single fishermen found it for her. As he clasped the necklace around her neck, he whispered sweet nothings into her ear. Later, the two would be seen fishing together at a private pond.

Answer Key
No Jumbling, page 14

Cat psychiatrists are busy these days because the stress placed upon pet cats has increased. People come home from work after a two-hour ride on the freeway, and pet cats demand attention. As soon as humans open the door, a pet cat is supposed to act fascinated and start purring. It doesn't matter to anyone that maybe the cat has been having a bad hairball day. The cat's feelings are totally ignored. It's only the whiny little humans that have real problems. After a few months of this treatment, most cats need therapy. Without it, they often end up on the streets, pushing a grocery cart and looking for pigeons that have bad coughs.

Armadillo Lil had a food stand that advertised a foot-long chili dog and fries for one dollar. Of course it was always crowded, which gave Lil a chance to show off her well-trained reptiles: an alligator, a snake, a turtle the size of a cantaloupe and a collection of Arizona lizards that did a great little trapeze act. Everything was fine until a stranger in a cowboy hat approached Lil's stand and accused her of selling "reptile chili."

Lil, who considered herself a great lover of animals, grew red in the face and glared at the stranger until he grew so nervous he took a few steps back.

"Sorry, ma'am," he said, tipping his hat. "I didn't mean that you actually do serve reptiles in your chili. I just wanted to point out that you *might as well*. These animals don't belong on some street corner turning cartwheels. They belong out in the desert running around and sitting on rocks in the sun. If you keep them here much longer, you'll make them so miserable you might as well put them in your chili."

Lil hated to admit it, but she knew he was right. That day, after she had served her last bowl of chili, she took all of the animals back to where she found them and let them go. Then she enrolled in a gymnastics class and learned how to do her own acrobatic tricks.

The cowboy became her biggest chili fan. Eventually, the two fell in love and got married. He even wore his cowboy hat to the wedding.

Answer Key
Starting and Stopping, page 16

The room was chilly when Rodney finally woke up. A shrill beep had been echoing in his dream for the past 20 minutes, but he couldn't force himself to open his eyes. Finally he did. The curtains were blowing across his desk, but the window was closed. A sharp blue light filled the room. When he turned back the covers of his bed, ten red Christmas tree ornaments with black legs marched up onto his pillow and started singing, "How Much Is That Doggie in the Window?"

Then Rodney got scared. He ran to the door, but it disappeared as he touched the knob. A voice said, "If you like tuna-melt sandwiches, follow us." Rodney followed. The little red people took him to a big sweaty warehouse filled with tables of cold cuts and wheat bread and tubs of tuna. The red creatures told him they were catering a UFO reunion to be held in Herbie Wartz's UFO Repair Shop on Thursday. If Rodney wanted to come, all he had to do was show up.

Suddenly the moon came out and beamed so brightly into his eyes that he had to dive back into bed and cover up his head. He didn't wake up until Thursday. He thought he'd had a nightmare until he saw tuna-melt crumbs on his pillow. Right then and there he decided to go to Herbie's UFO Repair Shop and check things out.

Rodney went inside the shop, even though the sign read, "Closed for a private party." About fifty little red people, who looked like the ones in Rodney's dream, were cheerfully munching on tuna melt sandwiches. When the little people saw Rodney, they let out a loud cheer. One of the people approached Rodney and smiled. "We were hoping you'd show up. We want you!"

"What for?" Rodney was starting to get scared. These guys were weird-looking.

"Herbie tells us you are the best swarzaphone player he knows, and we want you for Torkan Tunes, an intergalactic band. We travel around the galaxy performing concerts and promoting peace between the planets. What do you say?"

Rodney actually had nothing better to do. He was sick of folding little taco shells at Tiny Taco Town, and he couldn't get any music gigs because no one on earth understood his music. Finally, he had a chance to be appreciated. Rodney agreed to meet the Torkans at their spaceship the next day and go off with them for six Torkan months (or six Earth minutes). He thanked Herbie and vowed to always follow his dreams from now on.

DownWrite Funny © Taylor & Francis

Answer Key
Straightforward and Simple, page 18

1. The Prince of Slippers searched for Cindersmella.
2. An elf named Louise squeezed the lemon.
3. The last lonely alien phoned home.

Even though Frank was chubby, oafish and clumsy, he wanted to be a ballet dancer more than anything. He idolized Mikhail Baryshnikov, practiced his ballet moves every day and went to every ballet at the local Pickenteeth Theater. Frank dreamed of being a member of the Pointy Toe Ballet Troupe, but he always failed at the annual audition. Instead of giving up, he started his own ballet troupe so that he could be the director, choreographer and primo ballet dancer.

While anyone could admire Frank's determination and courage, no one could admire his first attempt at a ballet performance. Frank's one-man version of *Ballet Bambi* was a nightmare. He tried to play every role in the show, and the audience started looking forward to the time he took to change his costumes. According to one clever newspaper reporter, "Frank stank" as a ballet dancer

Lyle McCarthy, a local animal rights activist, said, "Frank's *Ballet Bambi* almost turned me into a blood-thirsty deer hunter." Mrs. Teerywater said, "This time I didn't cry only when Bambi's mom was killed. I cried through the entire show." One testy little bee hated the performance so much that he stung Frank during the "Flitting Flowers" number. Unruffled by the criticism, Frank continued his year-long tour of *Ballet Bambi*, playing to empty houses. Now he is working on his show for next year, *The Revenge of Tinkerbell.*

Answer Key
Active and Clear, page 20

1. Using a trampoline, Emilio leaped over short buildings.
2. The genie rubbed Mr. Marvin's bald head.
3. The door-to-door plunger salesman waited for Louise on the front porch.
4. Children who love its weird humor made *Space Rodents In Love* a hit movie.
5. Ms. Wooper saved expired cereal box tops.

__P__ Throughout the long, dark Halloween night, a complete buffalo costume was worn by Billie Beaker. __A__ He started his evening by gallumphing up to Mrs. Johnson's door and bellowing in his best buffalo impersonation, "Trick or treat!"

__P__ The door was opened by Mrs. Johnson. __P__ Lawn clippings were dropped into Billie's sack by her.

__A__ Billie went away feeling sad. __A__ He moaned deeply and sorrowfully. __A__ Just then, a real buffalo at the edge of town heard him.

__A__ At Mrs. Humblepup's house ten minutes later, something bumped Billie on the neck. __A__ He whirled around. __A__ A seven-foot buffalo stared down at him with bulging eyes full of buffalo sympathy and understanding. __P__ A scream was launched into the cold night air by Billie. __A__ He raced through Mrs. Humblepup's garden, flattening her scarecrow on the way out.

__P__ The sight of glowing buffalo eyes was never forgotten by Billie. __P__ The night light was kept on in his room until he was 18 years old.

Throughout the long, dark Halloween night, Billie Beaker wore a complete buffalo costume.
Mrs. Johnson opened the door.
She dropped lawn clippings into Billie's sack.
Billie launched a scream into the cold night air.
Billie never forgot the sight of glowing buffalo eyes.
He kept the night light on in his room until he was 18 years old.

Answer Key
To the Point, page 22

1. Humpty Dumpty's great-grandson sat on a bench.

2. A large, demented chicken looked for him.

The audience applauded as Madam Zorrino appeared on stage. Abby Tweed answered the call for a volunteer. Madam Zorrino placed Abby's hand into the Super Human Activator Device. The audience held its breath. Madam Zorrino furiously spun the crank on the machine.

Suddenly, Abby jerked her hand in an attempt to escape. With one big gulp, the Super Human Activator Device sucked terrified Abby right inside. The audience broke into a roaring applause, thinking that Madam Zorrino had performed a magnificent disappearing act. When the show finally ended two hours later, Madam Zorrino rescued Abby from the machine with a can opener. After that, Abby Tweed swore she would never volunteer for anything, anywhere, ever again.

Answer Key
On Purpose, page 24

1. Comfort
2. Teach
3. Scare
4. Invite
5. Entertain
6. Beg
7. Encourage

Single, fun-loving, brown and black basset hound with a gentle personality and a heart of gold seeks cute, slender French poodle, 21–35 in dog years. Must love frequent scratches behind the ears, lazy days on the porch and chasing Frisbees along the beach. Need not be athletic, but should enjoy short walks without leashes. Must love puppies.

Answer Key
A Goal in Mind, page 26

1. To apologize to the team.
2. To cheer the team up.
3. To criticize the team.
4. To instruct or guide the team.
5. To bribe the team.

We're only 50 points behind. Come on! That's not so bad! If we can score three points in the first half, we can surely score at least three more points in the second half! Even better than that, if we hold *them* to no points in the second half and score 50 ourselves, we will be tied and go into overtime. That's not impossible now, is it?

Gladiola, you guard that seven-foot seventh grader a little closer. Petunia, when that 200-pound blonde plows into you, hold your ground. Pansy, don't let Carmelo Anthony's daughter intimidate you when she leaps over your head to dunk the ball. Lily and Daisy, when those mean twin sisters yell at you as you shoot the ball, try not to drop it and run screaming toward the exits.

We can beat these wimps! Now come on, team. Let's go!

Answer Key
No Accidents, page 28

Graduation Day Speech:

Doctors, Frankensteins and other honored guests: We are living in an interesting era. It is only recently that "Frankenstein" has become a respected name in our society. People used to think of Frankensteins as oafish test-tube monsters that could barely speak, or else the results of some freakish science experiment gone bad. Thanks to great strides from historical Frankensteins and some English sheep cloners, genetically engineered beings can finally come out of the closet.

This is a great time to be a Frankenstein, and the future is bright. There are still the basic Hollywood jobs, of course—playing the original Frankenstein, doing monster voice-overs for Disney movies, adding a new angle to "Melrose Place" and standing in for the Jolly Green Giant. However, there are also a mass of *new* jobs opening up for young, bright Frankensteins like all of you. For example, genetic engineering is the perfect field for a Frankenstein. You have a personal feel for the subject unmatched by anyone. The U.S. Post Office is always looking for strapping strong young things to deliver the mail. Hardware store managers are also looking for Frankensteins to fill positions because so many of you are actually constructed from various hardware parts. Finally, the environmentalists are always looking for workers for their "It's Not Easy Being Green" campaign. With your coloring, you are perfect.

All in all, young Frankensteins, you can see that you've got the whole world in the palm of your green, grotesque, oversized hand, so go out there and make something of yourselves!

Answer Key
The Changing Audience, page 30

1. People hired to sell Sappy Sucker vacuum cleaners
2. A clerk at a store
3. Santa Claus
4. Oneself
5. The director of Camp Duckwaddle
6. A person's true love
7. "Trekkies" (Star Trek fans)
8. Audience at the taping of a television show
9. Students involved in an incident at a school
10. Someone learning to change a diaper

Answer Key
Working Together, page 32

1. Audience: New 4-H members. Purpose: to inform.
2. Audience: Young adults who love both computers and suspense. Purpose: to entertain.
3. Audience: Parents of teenagers. Purpose: to advise.

4. *Hospital Humor*
5. *The Barbie Blue Book*
6. *Rocking with the Oldies*

1. The *audience* is four very frightened kids on a camping trip.
2. The *purpose* of the piece of writing is to frighten the listeners.
3. As Evonna ran down the path, she could see a huge pair of bloodshot eyes staring at her through the trees. It was only a few more feet to the cabin. She pushed harder, trying to get to safety, and finally fell onto the door, gasping for breath. The door was stuck!

Answer Key
Just the "Write" Magazine, page 34

Title of magazine: "Ruffle Lover"

Audience profile: "Ruffle Lover" was started by Toots Flocklebee, an interior designer whose motto, "Rooms were made for ruffles," sums up the philosophy behind the magazine. Readers are women who just love decorating their homes and themselves with ruffles. Most readers are 35 to 60 years old, do not work outside the home and have the time and income to spend a lot of time decorating. They love to sew their own clothes, go square dancing and listen to country western stations.

Answer Key
Revealing Attitude, page 36

The following letter is written by a person who has decided to take an angry, threatening tone, hoping that the company will refund her money rather than deal with a lawsuit.

Oval V. Chip, President
Oatmeal Computer Company
Silikon Meadow, California 90522

Dear Mr. Chip:

The computer I purchased from you last month has just blown up in my face, singed my hair, knocked over my chocolate shake and shot a disc clear across the room, where it is now lodged in the wall!

Whoever put this computer together must have gruel for brains. I would rather eat cold porridge at every meal for the rest of my life than use one of your computers again. I am going to ship the pieces of this blown-up computer to each of the four corners of the world as a warning to others—unless you provide me with a skin graft, a wig, reimbursement for the chocolate shake, a new wall AND a refund! If you ask me, you are getting off easy.

I expect my refund to be in the mail tomorrow. I also expect an additional check for $12,622.72, to cover the estimated cost of the skin graft, wig, chocolate shake and the wall.

That should cover it. I expect you to comply with my request immediately, and you will be done with me. If you do not, I will turn the matter over to my billionaire lawyer brother-in-law, nicknamed "Pit Bull." (Hint: He didn't become a billionaire by losing lawsuits.)

Sincerely outraged,
Holly Hacker

P.S. Take me off your mailing list!

Answer Key
The Writer's Attitude, page 38

Friendly/Conversational Tone. Purpose: to share information with a friend
Dear Melanie,

What's up? Camp's been cooler than I thought it would be. It will be even better now that Herbert Harrison has been kicked out. You will not believe what he did this time. There's this guy, Rod, who's a counselor, and he is totally cute. He looks just like Edward Cullen in *Twilight*, plus he is totally nice. And you know how Herbert is always playing jokes on people. Well, he dropped worms in Rod's mouth while he was sleeping. Rod woke up right away, or who knows what could have happened. Anyway, it all turned out for the best because Herbert got a one-way ticket out of Camp Duckwaddle for good. I have to close now—time for lights out. I'll see you when I come home, and I'll let you know if anything happens between Rod and me. Keep your fingers crossed.

Love,
Angie

Formal Tone. Purpose: to notify parents of child's expulsion

Dear Mr. and Mrs. Harrison:

This letter serves as official notification that your son Herbert Harrison is being discharged from our camp immediately. Yesterday afternoon Herbert violated several camp rules and, more seriously, was the instigator in an incident involving the reckless endangerment of a camp counselor. We have chosen not to press charges at this time, provided that your son is removed from camp as soon as possible, no later than Wednesday, August 15. In addition, you are hereby notified that Herbert Harrison is forever prohibited from attending or visiting any of the nationwide Camp Duckwaddles, for any reason whatsoever.

Sincerely,
Norma Risenhover
Director, CampDuckwaddle

Hysterical Tone. Purpose: to vent

Dear Miss Risenhover:

My daughter has informed me of the horrible incident that happened yesterday involving a camp counselor, and I am worried to death about the safety of my daughter and everyone else attending Camp Duckwaddle! It's just awful what Herbert did to that poor counselor! Can't a person get sick from swallowing worms? The poor man had to have his stomach pumped, I'm sure, and he's bound to get a big bill from the hospital. Who knows if he even has insurance? Since camp counselors don't make that much money, he probably doesn't. What in the world is his family going to do if they have to pay for all that? You know, I think that the hospital should send that bill to Herbert's parents, and they should make sure Herbert works to pay it off. That kid should never be allowed to attend any camp in this country again! In fact, I think he should be grounded by his parents until he is at least 21!

With worry and concern,
Ella May MacTavish

Critical Tone. Purpose: to complain

Dear Miss Risenhover:

Herbert Harrison has got to be the most thoughtless, brutish, cruel camper ever to attend Camp Duckwaddle. His idea of a joke just plain insults the intelligence of the counselors. What was he doing trespassing in a counselor's cabin, anyway? He had no business being there, and it's just a good thing he was caught. Camp Duckwaddle personnel should be more careful about who they allow into the camp. I'm afraid all of us are needlessly endangered by children like this.

Sincerely,
Walter Glormer, Camp Counselor

Answer Key
Diplomacy Counts, page 40

1. Your smile is such a pleasant diversion that I couldn't possibly concentrate on my food.
2. Your neighbors must find it difficult to match your standard of living.
3. Would you like to borrow my mud mask and radish weed skin toner for the next decade?
4. You are very down-to-earth.

To: Manfred@swampmail.com

Manfred, it's not that you have done something that is so terrible. These past six months have been fun, but I think that you and I are from different parts of the swamp. You know, I am more of an upstream girl, and you are just a good old downstream kind of guy. While I'm sure there are thousands of other female alligators that would love a guy who pats his overstuffed belly and picks his teeth with a bone after dinner, I'm not one of them.

You see, Manfred, it's not you; it's me. I'm the one with the problem. I'm the one who can't get beyond your adorable yet annoying honk of a laugh. And everyone *else* laughs at all your jokes. You're a laid back guy without a care in the world, and I'm just different. You know, Manfred, you deserve someone that will appreciate the way you sing show tunes off key at the top of your lungs and the way that you boyishly frolic in the filthy, mosquito-infested mud of the shore. Manfred, there are more fish in the sea. You and I, however, just aren't meant to be.

Lady Myrtle's little pet dragon Maynard had been dragging his tail ever **since** the drawbridge accident, **so** she decided to perk him up by putting him to work. **Because** it was such a beautiful, leaf-scented spring day, she decided he should come outside **and** help her plant a garden.

First, Maynard waddled ahead of her, making nifty furrows in the soft dirt with his damaged tail. **Then** Lady Myrtle, addicted to turnips **and** full of joy, waltzed behind, casting seed onto the ground in neat, zippy rows.

There was a problem, **however.** Lady Myrtle soon saw that she couldn't wear slippers in the garden **because** it was so muddy. Sir Bernie often came up to the fence by the garden, hoping that someone would offer him a free squash. The problem? Everyone knew that if a knight saw a lady's bare feet, he would have to propose marriage— whether he loved her or not.

On this particular spring day, Lady Myrtle saw no sign of Sir Bernie, **so** she took off her slippers and con- tinued planting. **While** she worked, **though,** Sir Bernie walked up to the fence and leaned against it, dreaming of luscious vegetables. Maynard sensed his presence **and** started growling. Lady Myrtle, who didn't know what was wrong at first, put Maynard on his leash.

Since Maynard hated knights, his nostrils started to flare. Red smoke wafted up in the form of a smoky little flame that didn't scare anybody. Lady Myrtle jerked on Maynard's leash, causing him to hiccup **and** shoot an arc of flame in Sir Bernie's direction. **Immediately** the scene grew tense.

Maynard accidentally spewed flames at Sir Bernie **and** burnt his tongue in the process. **While** most dragons could handle the pain of a burnt tongue, Maynard was a complete wimp. **At first** he tried screaming, **but** his swol- len tongue wouldn't allow him to continue. **Eventually** he started to run around the garden in an attempt to cool off his tongue. **Because** Lady Myrtle had her hands entwined in the leash, she was dragged behind. **As** her pointy hat plowed through the mud **and** her flailing body destroyed many of the plants, her dress flew over her head in a very unladylike way. **Thus,** her bare feet weren't the only things she was in danger of revealing to Sir Bernie. He was **also** likely to see her twelve petticoats and flowered bloomers.

Not to worry, **however**—Sir Bernie suddenly became the most gallant of knights. Covering his eyes, he rushed onto the scene. Using his newfound good sense, he persuaded the raving dragon to stop his frenzied gallop. **As** Maynard slowed down, Sir Bernie grabbed a large onion sack that rested in the garden. **When** Maynard came to a halt, he sent Lady Myrtle flying across the field. Quickly, Bernie used the onion sack to catch the poor lady. He put her in the shade to rest **and then** used his Swiss army knife to cut cool cucumber slices to lay on the dragon's throbbing tongue. **After** 45 minutes, Maynard's tongue was back to its normal size. Sir Bernie had saved the day.

A little-known rule stated that anytime a lady **and** her dragon were rescued by a knight, she had to propose marriage to him—whether she loved him or not. Lady Myrtle proposed to Sir Bernie, **and** Sir Bernie proposed to her. (He *had* seen her feet.) They were married the very next day in a beautiful ceremony. At the reception, every- one feasted on chef salads and chocolate zucchini cake.

Last night, I went into the kitchen, quietly. I opened the cupboard **and** got out a mousetrap. **First,** I spread open the wire bar on the trap. **Next,** I put in a piece of cucumber smeared with peanut butter. **After** I set the trig- ger of the trap, I gently laid it on the shelf under the sink. **As** I closed the cupboard door under the sink, I heard the trap snap shut. I was afraid to look under the sink, **so** I went back to bed. **However,** I had nightmares about mouse homicide court.

The most exciting thing that ever happened to the citizens of Dullsburg was opening their mail every day. Therefore, they were very upset when they stopped receiving any mail at all—not even junk mail. This went on for two weeks, and the people were baffled and angry.

Then one day Marty Moranski walked by the post office and saw a **creature** in the parking lot munching on mail. Marty ran home and told his parents he had seen a sticky, slimy, rainbow-colored **monster** as big as a mailbox with letters stuck to its body. Marty's parents told the police to investigate the **organism** to see if it was dangerous. When the police arrived with their nets, the **freak** smiled at them, opening a huge mouth full of catalogs, letters to "occupant" and "two for one" coupons for pizza.

"Why, this **fiend** is a junk mail junkie!" cried Sergeant Stubb.

"I believe this **living thing** evolved because there is just too much junk mail to fit in our mailboxes," declared Professor Dryman. "Let's feed it all it can eat."

"No, no," cried Ms. Dresswright. "That **gargoyle** ate a month's worth of my favorite catalogs."

Everyone who was watching the **beast** started to argue. Finally the Dullsburg City Council decided that the **animal** would live at the local zoo. People would bring their junk mail, after they were finished with it, for "Sticky" to eat.

Answer Key
Connecting with Pronouns, page 48

Seymour was walking home from school through the park when **he** heard a whimpering sound coming from behind a bush. Huddled in the bush was a little winged hippopotamus. **It** looked at **him** and continued to whimper. **He** heard the same whimpering sound coming from above **his** head. **He** looked up and saw two more winged hippos peering over the edge of a nest. "That's something you don't see very often," **he** thought.

The hippo on the ground gazed up at the nest and whimpered even louder. Seymour felt really sorry for the little guy and decided to carry **him** up to the nest. **He** hoisted the heavy hippo over **his** shoulder and climbed the tree, grunting from the strain. After **he** deposited the hippo in the nest and climbed down, **he** glanced overhead just in time to see a huge mother hippo flying towards the nest. **She** looked angry.

Seymour decided it was time to leave. The last thing in the world **he** wanted was to be confronted by a two-ton flying animal protecting **her** babies.

Answer Key
Three in One, page 50

Pecos Pete walked into the town of Tulip just before sundown. **He** set his laptop computer on the Tomb of the Unknown Grocer and said, "My **machine** can whip any dimwitted, hot-wired, battery-powered **piece of electronics** in this town."

First the people were frightened. **Then** one small lady from the U-Name It shop said, "My **PeachPit 5000** will beat **yours** with three minutes to spare, **or** you can have every close-out coupon I've got in my purse."

Pecos Pete roared, "I'm the laptopping-est, smooth typing-est, rip-roarin' digital sound byting-est **critter** that ever typed a memo. You're on, **Missy**."

The contest lasted two hours.

Finally, the mayor declared the **competition** closed. "The winner **and** computing champion is **Ms. Mulldoop!**"

Pecos Pete's new laptop computer was coughing and wheezing like a tired horse. **He** was sweating like a dishrag. "All right, lady, you win," **he** said. "But be prepared to lose next time. Then I'll bring my handbook along **and also** a friend of mine from Texas who can read!"

Mr. Anderson had read in a book that you should always hang your cooler in a nearby tree when camping. Supposedly, hanging it in a tree will keep you and your food safe from wild animals—*most* wild animals, that is. The book did not take into account the talented bear cousins, Boffo, Bombo and Binky.

Boffo is a seven-foot bear who enjoys drinking sodas, playing games and observing the natural behavior of Homo sapiens, or man. He had just completed a night course called Studies of the North American Man at the local community college with his cousins, Bombo and Binky, when they stumbled upon the Andersons' campsite.

"A piñata!" thought Boffo when he saw the cooler hanging in the tree. Known for loving games, he excitedly wrapped the Andersons' new table cloth around his head. Then he whacked at the little refrigerator box with a nearby stick. The playful beast pounded and hit and beat the cooler until he woke up the Anderson family, which excited Binky immensely. "Finally, an opportunity to study a terrified family of Homo sapiens!" exclaimed Binky as he began snapping photographs.

Nine-foot tall Bombo heard something rustling in the undergrowth and went to check it out. Suddenly something went screaming past him and climbed onto the roof of the camper. It was a horrified and quivering Mr. Anderson, who must have been taking a midnight stroll when the three cousins rolled into camp. "Get a picture of the cornered Homo sapiens, Binky," said Bombo.

At last, Boffo cracked open the cooler. Hamburgers, hotdogs and marshmallows spilled from it. The bears were disappointed to see there was no candy, though. After feasting on camp grub and taking dozens of photos of the Anderson family, the cousins lumbered off.

The next day, while the Andersons slept at the local Holiday Inn, the three bears submitted their photographs to the local Wilderness Gazette. Mr. Anderson later found his picture on the front page of the newspaper, looking horrified and white as a ghost. The caption read, "Don't hang your cooler in a tree."

Answer Key
In Focus, page 52

Hanna saw things that other people didn't see. During a slumber party one night, for example, she saw the shadow of an arm holding a gun. She screamed, "Duck! Fast! Before we're all shot to death!" After her friends' hearts started beating again, they looked at the shadow Hanna pointed out to them. They saw the shadow of a tree branch, not an arm with a gun.

Another time, she looked at the sweet plum preserves that the 70-year-old neighbor down the block gave to her. She was sure she saw blood and the top of a thumb in the jar. While she waited for her mother to come home, so that she could tell her about it, Hanna decided to keep an eye on Mrs. Nelms, who was working in her garden. "She's digging a place for the rest of the body!" she thought to herself. She was just about to call the police when her mother came home. Her mother frowned at Hanna, shook her head and opened the jar of preserves. There were plenty of pieces of plum in the jar, but no thumb.

One day Hanna was outside the teachers' lounge when she heard her English teacher talking on the phone. "Meet me in my classroom at 3:15," said Mr. Dutton in a low voice. She peeked into the room and saw Mr. Dutton folding up a piece of paper and putting it in his pocket. "He's a spy!" thought Hanna, remembering the trench coat he often wore and his shifty eyes. (At least she thought they were shifty now.) She decided that she would save the United States from this evil spy.

At 3:15 she waited outside Mr. Dutton's classroom. Sure enough, a thin woman dressed in black showed up and slipped into the room. Mr. Dutton handed her the piece of paper from his pocket. Thinking quickly, Hanna pulled the fire alarm and yelled, "Citizen's arrest! I'm making a citizen's arrest!"

Mr. Dutton looked at her as if she were crazy. So did the principal, seven teachers and the members of the fire department who showed up a short time later.

The woman in black opened up her purse and showed everyone the note Mr. Dutton had given her. It said, "Optometrist. 1463 Penrose Place. Insurance #2657923." Mr. Dutton looked at Hanna. "My wife is taking our son to get his eyes checked. I wrote down the address and insurance number for her, and she stopped by to pick up our check book."

Mr. and Mrs. Dutton, the principal, the seven teachers and the fire fighters all glared at Hanna. She turned red with humiliation.

She decided right then and there to keep the strange things she imagined to herself.

Answer Key
UnCool, page 53

"Crunch, slurp, chomp!" Blitzen sits in his apartment eating a gorp-like mixture of mistletoe, grass and Mrs. Claus' chocolate fudge that he sneaks out of her refrigerator in the middle of the night. He is wearing dark shades, a tank top and striped boxer shorts. Between his gigantic antlers grows a tuft of hair that he combs straight up and hairsprays stiff. An earring dangles from his left ear.

Blitzen's apartment is a bachelor's delight. A picture of his beautiful reindeer girlfriend sits on top of the television. A basketball hoop hangs on his wall, and he always has a basketball nearby so that he can toss a few baskets between commercials. He doesn't have any lamps because of all that hoop-shooting during commercials.

Blitzen bops his head back and forth to tunes from his iPod while he watches a reindeer boxing match on Channel 2. He flips between the boxing and his favorite episode of "Holiday Idol" on Channel 4.

Soon Blitzen will have to get off the couch and head to band practice. He is the lead jingler in the Jingle Bell Band. He has dozens of girls (both human and reindeer) hanging around, hoping to get a date with him. He hardly notices.

Answer Key
"Awesome" Isn't Good Enough, page 55

Mollie's pet goldfish are shy. Actually, they aren't even gold. They are dull orange. They have large fanning tails that spread out gracefully through the water when they swish them. The two goldfish don't do very much—at least not when they know you're looking at them. They just hide behind their plants and blow bubbles that remind you of a string of pearls. If you don't clean their aquarium every week, they start smelling like old linoleum in the kitchen of a seafood restaurant.

Answer Key
Simple Similes, page 56

Shy Goldfish

Bill Sapp:	You've never been on our show. Thanks for stopping by.
Miss Muffet:	I'm as thrilled as <u>a grand-prize winning contestant on "The Price Is Right"</u> to be here.
Bill Sapp:	Well, isn't that nice. Let's begin with what I'm sure is a difficult topic for you. Tell our audience how you became addicted to cheese.
Miss Muffet:	I was young and as dumb as <u>a sparrow flirting with a tomcat</u> when I first came to my grandparents' farm in upstate New York.
Bill Sapp:	We know that. We all read the poem about you being terrified of a stupid spider.
Miss Muffet:	That spider wasn't stupid. He was as smart as <u>Albert Einstein on brain pills</u>.
Bill Sapp:	Well, fine. But what about your cheese addiction?
Miss Muffet:	That came much later, on a night that was as dark as <u>my bedroom closet and just as scary</u>.
Bill Sapp:	Skip the weather reports. Have you beaten the addiction? Are you free from the power of cheese?
Miss Muffet:	I was never addicted to cheese. It was the *whey* that I was so fond of. I enjoyed whey as much as <u>a grandma</u> enjoys <u>grabbing her favorite grandchild and smothering her with kisses.</u>
Bill Sapp:	Did the spider get you hooked? Is that why you were afraid of him?
Miss Muffet:	I was NOT afraid of him. I was allergic. His crept up next to me as silently as <u>a teenager sneaking in after curfew,</u> and I broke out in hives.
Bill Sapp:	So you didn't leave your little sitting stool because you were frightened?
Miss Muffet:	No. I'm not the kind of girl to be pushed off a stool. The hives made me as itchy as <u>wool long johns on the Fourth of July</u>. I had to run or go mad.
Bill Sapp:	You seem well now.
Miss Muffet:	I'm fit as a fiddle.
Bill Sapp:	That's a rather weak simile for a girl as talented as you.
Miss Muffet:	Okay. I'm as fit as <u>the four-time reigning champion of the universe-wide aerobic competition.</u>

Answer Key
Metaphorically Speaking, page 58

I was at K-mart when an announcer spoke over the intercom: "All customers please assemble in the center of the store. A tornado is approaching." **Shopping quickly became a nightmare. I was a turtle scurrying for cover** as I dipped under a table of mouthwash on sale for $1.29. I shivered and shook. **My mouth was a dry dishcloth. My tongue was a Brillo pad. My toes were claws** gripping the inside of my Himalayan hiking boots, on special for $31.95 if you bought two pair.

Suddenly the flashing blue light in the panty hose aisle fizzled. The store lights went black. The **place became a tomb of silence.** I thought of all the shopping I would never do, all the blue-light specials I would miss. Then the lights snapped on and the announcer said, "Sorry for the scare, folks. The tornado went south."

I danced. I sang. **I was a ballerina in hiking boots.** I had faced the **monster** and survived. I would live to shop another day.

Albert: But I want to be near you, my sweet Rice Krispies Treat.
Madge: Though your arms are soft fresh Twinkies, I don't want to muss my hair.
Albert: Ah, your hair! It is fluffy, full, spun cotton candy.
Madge: Why Albert, you smooth, chocolate mocha milk shake!
Albert: Your presence is a bowlful of fruity Skittles after a dreary meal.
Madge: I know our love will never become a soggy, stale three-day-old Whopper.
Albert: Never, my tasty little Snickers bar!

Answer Key
Word Magic, page 60

Maple Street #1—warmth of rising sun, children running their bikes, mothers pushing infants in strollers, business people opening shops and setting out tables, good cup of coffee
Maple Street #2—wind whipped; cold cobbled surface; empty cans rattling; clinking, hollow bells; echoing loneliness and fear; no one, not a single soul; graveyard; stiff benches where no one sat

Living room #1

The living room glows with the warmth of an inviting fire. The soft Manx kitten purrs comfortably on the window sill, protected from the cool breeze outside. Delicate brown and gold leaves drift to the ground outside, where they dance and tumble over one another like kittens. The plump pillows in the easy chair are fluffed to cozy perfection. One book rests on a cushion, another on the floor, both waiting for a someone to curl up and read them.

Living room #2

A frigid wind howls outside, threatening to rush down the chimney and throw a spark of deadly fire onto the aged pages of an unread book. The spindly branches of the old oak tree scratch at the window as the kitten meows nervously, watching for owners who are late coming home. Articles of clothing that have long lost the warmth of the bodies that wore them lay strewn about the house, discarded and uncared for. Yellowed flowers on the table tremble and shiver as a gust of wind fills the room and rattles the glass pane of the front window.

Answer Key
Getting Rid of the Gray, page 62

1. Spring break in Yellowstone was exciting because I rode there on the back of a Harley, stayed up late to eat s'mores around the campfire every night and watched a bear wearing a backpack wander through our camp site.
2. My hamburger smelled like dirty sweat socks and wiggled like rubber, and my french fries were stiff with hardened lard.
3. The party was more boring than a math quiz because all the guests were my parents' age, the music was "geezer rock," and the only foods served were low-fat dips and salt-free Triscuits.
4. Every morning while my dad wrestles with our Saint Bernard and my brother slaps peanut butter on Wonder

Bread for his lunch and complains loudly that Mom and Dad "never let him do anything fun," my baby brother howls as he flings his mushy Fruit Loops all over the floor.

Answer Key
Face It, page 64

Glue Boy's face is oval-shaped, and his skin is so pale you can almost see the veins around his temples. His hair is short and brown, with the word "Elmer" shaved into the back just above the nape of his neck. His eyes are glassy blue and look very innocent. His nose is hooked and has marks on each side of the bridge from wearing glasses or sunglasses. His nostrils are large. His lips are rosy, rubbery and almost always curling up. His eyebrows are arched and look like they have been waxed. His eyelashes are brown and curled. As for his ears, they are Spock-like. They look fake, like they are made of plastic. He has no earlobes. His chin is pink and fleshy with three warts. His forehead protrudes like a caveman's, and his neck is short and stocky. As for his teeth, they are small, white and perfectly straight. He must have a good dentist.

Answer Key
Common Sense, page 66

Note: some words may fit reasonably into more than one category. Here is one breakdown:

Sound	Taste	Touch	Sight	Smell
squawk	sour	smooth	red	sour
hissing	salty	slimy	smooth	acrid
scream	moldy	unpainted	short	salty
honk	spicy	scratchy	slimy	musty
toot	delicious	scaly	unpainted	moldy
purr	scrumptious	sticky	moldy	spicy
sizzle	pungent	oily	tilted	rank
moan	cheesy	creamy	scaly	delicious
croak	oily	dusty	rounded	sulphurous
yowl	lemony	moist	oval	scrumptious
screech	peppery	icy	skinny	pungent
tweet	sweet	clammy	pitted	oily
whine	bitter	soggy	oily	aromatic
roar	nutty	humid	curved	lemony
bark	creamy		wavy	peppery
bleat	moist		gray-haired	sweet
jingling	rotten		straight	bitter
banging	smoky		triangular	nutty
snapping			pointy	dusty
crackling			dusty	rotten
popping			rotten	smoky
			icy	fragrant

Oval-headed Ollie is attempting to eliminate the sour taste in his mouth by eating a soggy mound of pancakes drenched in sticky syrup. The bee hovering in the background is attracted to the sweet smelling mound and has plans to get Ollie out of the way. If Ollie continues to ignore the whine of the bee over his shoulder, he is sure to yowl in pain when he feels the stinger plunge into his skin. The red, pointy welt that will develop should be enough to send Ollie screaming to his mother, leaving the pancakes unguarded.

Answer Key
Virtual Reality, page 68

Situation #2. It's funny. I'm sitting here on the moon, and all I can think about is my Aunt Edna. There is just something about the moon that reminds me of visiting her.

First of all, the temperature on the moon changes as fast as Aunt Edna's moods. One minute I'm so cold that my shivering is rattling my oversized space suit and clanking the metal clips on my moon boots. When I walk into the sunlight, however, I'm so hot that my skin flushes magenta, and my pores gush oceans of salty sweat. After that, my suit smells like a sick concoction of sweat and vinyl.

Also, the crunchy, sticky feel of this plastic space suit reminds me of peeling my bare summer legs off of Aunt Edna's plastic-covered pink couch. The flaky gray, ash-like moon dust looks and feels like Aunt Edna's skin, while the obnoxious orange glow of the sun matches the color of Aunt Edna's dyed beehive hairdo. The sparkling twinkle of the Milky Way is reminiscent of Aunt Edna's authentic rhinestone jewels. As I'm struck with all the memories of Aunt Edna, I look at the earth and wonder if I ever want to go back.

Describe what is happening in the picture below: Winifred the Rat thought she had found paradise. Actually, she had discovered a closet shelf where a young woman had stashed away all the remnants of her girlhood. There were many nooks to hide in, stuffed animals to play with and, best of all, a bright plastic jack-o-lantern basket filled with trick-or-treat goodies.

When Winifred made the candy discovery, she could not believe her good luck and immediately began to feast on the forgotten sweets. She did not know, however, that the girl had stowed away all this stuff when she turned 11—and the girl was now 17. Winifred just scarfed things down so quickly that she didn't realize that much of the candy was old, stale or even rotten. One second she was licking a strawberry and banana swirled sucker with green fuzz on it, and the next she was popping stale SweeTarts that tasted bitter. As she tried to sink her teeth into a soft, chewy caramel, Winifred almost chipped a molar on the not-so-fresh candy. Then she gobbled up a York Peppermint Patty so fast that she didn't even notice that it was so old it tasted more like an old bike tire than peppermint.

Finally, after she had gobbled the last morsel of concrete grape Laffy Taffy, Winifred looked down and noticed that her bloated gray belly was doing the hula all on its own. All at once her tummy stopped moving and turned into one enormous stomach cramp. Jolted by the pain, Winifred gasped, wrapped her fat little rodent claws around her overstretched belly button and collapsed onto a discarded avocado green wool sweater.

Answer Key
Generic Images, page 70

1. The flimsy gray rags of clothing whipped in the wind around the stout little woman as she trudged behind her frosty metal grocery cart through two feet of snow, heading toward the chicken-noodle smell of the soup kitchen one block over.

2. The old, yellowing books lay scattered on rickety tables in the silent shadows of the cold, musty library.

3. Unable to stand up to the July heat, the three big scoops of sticky mint chocolate chip ice cream melted down the cone and wound around my sweaty wrist.

4. Graffiti stained the deserted walls of the subway, and the smell of sweat and wet wool leaked from the ripped vinyl seats and cracked floors.

5. The cracked helmets, broken sticks and torn jerseys that littered the locker room told the story of a bloody hockey game on the ice outside.

That rotten little beagle of mine was grinning from ear to ear, perching on my briefcase like a spoiled canary. He crawled up there just before the cloudburst and got himself safely under some kid's umbrella. He panted softly while the rain landed in tiny plunks on the umbrella. I shivered as the raindrops soaked into my clothes and the smell of wet wool settled around my nose.

Answer Key
Details for Atmosphere, page 72

A sloppy atmosphere—

As I opened the door, the smell from the **basket of decaying sweat socks** hit me. Behind me, on the wall, hung a **Nerf basketball hoop,** the net dangling by two or three threads. I stepped over the **cracked blue football helmet,** only to trip on **Rollerblades** and fall flat on my back. I looked up and saw a row of **gold trophies,** some upright, some knocked over. As I sat up, I decided to be more careful where I walked. The **mini-tv/DVD** had been left on, and a **DVD** was playing a show about funny sports bloopers. **A Wilson tennis racket** and a box of bright yellow **Dunlop tennis balls** lay on top of the yellow and blue **San Diego Chargers bedspread.** I suddenly became light-headed from the odors and made a dash for the door, leaping over a cardboard **box overflowing with baseball cards** and narrowly missing a deflated **black and white soccer ball.** I yanked open the door and breathed deeply.

A "frilly" atmosphere—

I opened the **pale pink door** at the end of the hall and smelled the fragrance of lilacs in a **glass vase.** The **pink walls** were hung with **posters of bright, blooming flowers.** The **pink and white eyelet lace curtains** were open, and a light breeze wafted through the window. The **pale pink floral bedspread** was decorated with **lacy floral pillows,** and a **kitty cat clock** smiled at me. On top of the **whitewashed dresser** was a **delicate music box.** I opened it, and the ballerina popped up and danced to the twinkling tune of Michael Bolton's "Love Is a Wonderful Thing." Next to the music box lay two **dainty heart-shaped necklaces** and some **sparkling earrings** made of silver and gold. From the corner of the room, I could hear classical music playing in the **CD player.**

Answer Key
Focal Points, page 74

I first saw it out of the corner of my eye as it slithered slowly across the kitchen floor. Its one bulging eye stood above its body and stared straight ahead. The eye was attached to a round, ugly, wet, cream-colored body about the size of a golf ball. The blobby body scraped on the ground as the insect moved. A hard, black shovel-shaped horn stuck out from the front of the creature to scoop up everything in its path—like dust balls, crumbs and small bugs. On the back of the blob was a long pointed tail that pushed the blob along the ground. The tail was covered with dark, stiff green scales.

The scene was so disgusting that I wanted to throw up, but instead I just squashed the blob under my shoe. The squashed insect left a greenish puddle of ooze on the floor and on the bottom of my shoe. I promptly threw away my shoes and left the mess for my brother to clean up.

Answer Key
Focus Attention, page 76

When I first looked at the statue honoring cranky librarians, I couldn't take my eyes off her face. She had small, menacing eyes that followed me around wherever I walked. The eyes asked sternly, "How many days late? What kind of damage? Don't you know how to use the *Reader's Guide to Periodical Literature?*" Her eyebrows slanted forward in exasperation. Her thin smile was a gash in the granite. Miniature book earrings dangled from her earlobes. Her granite hair was pulled back into a severe bun that was anchored to the top of her skull.

Her head sat atop a skinny, wrinkly neck. Her neck was mostly concealed by a high collared blouse fringed with lace. Ivory buttons ran down the front of the conservative blouse, and she clutched an armload of books protectively.

Her heavy-looking skirt fell almost to the soles of her sturdy shoes. The tips of the shoes came to a sharp point, making it look as though her granite toes had to be scrunched painfully together.

Answer Key
Step by Step, page 78

Ms. Huff has been the school secretary for at least 165 years, and her hairdo has never changed, except for the color. I have often wondered what could be inside that ancient pile of gray and silver. One day I happened to catch her napping at her desk, so I tiptoed in to get to the bottom of the mystery.

First I removed the red and white polka-dotted bow at the top of her tall stack of hair. **Then** I pushed the top layers of hair out of the way. The twisted tangle of hair was difficult to maneuver through, but I managed.

Next I reached into my pocket and pulled out a comb. I used it to help me make my way through the layers of gray frizz and fluff. **Halfway through** I saw the hair moving and heard a buzzing sound. **Farther on,** as my arm was disappearing up to my elbow, I felt a sudden sharp pain. Something had stung me! I quickly shoved the frizzy mass to the side and looked closer. **Finally,** the mystery was solved. Ms. Huff truly had a beehive hairdo. There was a beehive inside!

I tried to rearrange the hair back on top of her head. Then I headed for the nurse's office to have her remove the stinger the bee had left in my arm.

Answer Key
Too Much of a Good Thing, page 80

Trek to Mount Oregano

The ~~tired~~ weary group continued trudging ~~and marching~~ through the dense ~~thick~~ jungle, looking for the lost city of Pasta. It was getting dark. As Pamela climbed Mount Oregano, she could hear far-off ~~distant~~ drums. The sound sent chills up her spine. She ~~shivered and~~ said, "Rupert, bring me the big ~~giant~~ squirt gun."

The path was so overgrown that Pamela couldn't see anything ahead of her. She loaded the squirt gun with diet ~~sugar-free~~ soda and squeezed the trigger. Immediately the green leaves on the bushes turned brown and fell off. ~~The path cleared.~~ Pamela and her troupe proceeded until they came to an ancient ~~old~~ shrine. It was an important ~~special~~ moment. The group was getting ~~nearer and~~ closer to the lost city.

"We must go on," Pamela urged. Suddenly, there was a shout…

"Who goes there? And don't you know you shouldn't bring diet soda anywhere near Italian food?" queried a gruff voice.

Pamela turned to the voice and saw a small man in beach wear. "We, uh, are looking for the lost city of Pasta. Do you know where it is?"

"Do I know where it is? I *live* there. *Of course* I know where it is. Follow me."

Pamela and her friends followed the man into town. Except for the jungle atmosphere, Pasta looked a lot like Pamela's own home town back in Michigan. Soon the group reached the town square, where a big celebration was taking place.

Flags waved from poles on top of buildings, bright banners bounced on wires stretched across the street and people everywhere danced to a lively drumbeat. The air was filled with the sweet smell of basil mixed with garlic. Pamela knew her party's hard trek through the wilderness was worth the effort when she threw aside her squirt gun and sat down to devour a heaping plate of spaghetti.

Answer Key
Description Out of Whack, page 82

He slipped into the dark kitchen on a moonlit summer night and tip-toed up to the refrigerator ~~in his new African hunting shoes that were as brown as fawn skin with bright green laces that looked like they had been dyed using real lime peels~~. The Cheese Muncher gently pulled open the door, ~~which was as white as ice cream, smooth and shiny, with that just-wiped look of a door that is ready to get its picture taken~~. The light inside the fridge was out, so the Cheese Muncher flicked on his ~~multi-use underwater galactic~~ flashlight ~~that was made by artistically challenged people in Seattle, a lovely place to visit in summer if you like to watch whales in the harbor spouting silver cascades of water~~.

He probed the refrigerator with the beam of his flashlight and found that every single thing in it was moldy. Most people would think that all that mold was gross. The Cheese Muncher, however, thought he was in heaven. After all, cheese actually *is* mold. He loved the green fuzzy growth on the carrots. He savored the gray fur on the edges of the bread. His mouth watered for the cottony white fuzz on the broccoli at the back of the fridge, but just as he grabbed it, he heard footsteps in the hallway. He quickly shut off his flashlight, stuffed the fuzzy broccoli in his mouth and slipped out the back door. He knew he would be hitting this house again in about a month, when all the family's food had rotted again.

Answer Key
Overdone, page 84

Enjoy the glorious sound of your close-knit family harmonizing in celebration over your special day of birth into this wondrous world. Bask in the glow of an oversized frosting-coated cake, brilliant with the light of sparkling candles that add elegant ambiance to your celebration.

As you bite into the sweet tenderness of Rocky Road Mud Pie, inhale the complex scents of gooey marshmallow and minty chocolate filling. You will appreciate the artistically placed mound of melting French vanilla ice cream that drips dramatically to the plate.

The lavishly landscaped Downtown Park affords a plethora of exercise experiences for you and your dog, whether it be a casual romp with the Frisbee or a brisk run along the bicycle trail at sunset. You and your dog will enjoy frolicking in this beautiful outdoor setting as you marvel at the majestic city skyline on the horizon.

Answer Key
Plain Silly, page 86

1. She scolded him for moving his hands like a monkey when he talked.
2. A person should never lie.
3. Nothing's worse than a pregnant elephant at a party.
4. The elves worked hard for two weeks without pay.
5. Viola trapped the robber in her bathroom and yelled at him.
6. Pecos Sal's weakened horse wouldn't walk any farther.

Good morning, Earthlings. I want to thank all of you for coming out here today and supporting me. When my assistant saw that it was raining all over the galaxy this morning, he feared no one would show up for this rally. But Earthlings, let me tell you, that thought never crossed my mind. I knew you would be here. I knew you would want to show your support for the best candidate for the District 4 Galaxy Council. Why am I the best candidate? Because I support better schools and better school lunches. Because I will clean up our streets and put dangerous criminals in jail. Because I am committed to helping the poor and the homeless. Because I will lead the fight to put Internet access into the nursing homes and get all those nice people online. Citizens of Earth, you knew what kind of woman you want sitting on that Council, and that is why you came out here to see me today. Thank you.

The day breaks grandly, Nitt-Wittians. I would like to solemnly express my extreme gratitude to all of you for being present and providing me with emotional sustenance in this twenty-four-hour period. At the moment my assistant became cognizant of the fact that there existed a veritable deluge throughout the galaxy, he became overwhelmed with trepidation. Timorous, he shivered with the uncertainty about whether or not any of you would grant me your presence at this assemblage. But Nitt-Wittians, that particular speculation did not even exist for one nanosecond within the realm of my consciousness. I was certain of your attendance. I was cognizant of your commitment to supporting the most appropriate candidate the District 4 Galaxy Council has ever encountered. Why am I the most appropriate candidate? Because I want to improve pedagogical institutions and provide more delectable cuisine in those institutions, as well. Because I want to rid our thoroughfares of malefactors and place them in punitive correctional facilities separate from the rest of society proper. Because I am devoted to providing succor to those suffering pecuniary privation and to those lacking satisfactory domiciles. Because I am the key proponent of providing Internet access to those inhabitants residing in abodes designed especially for the aged and getting those septuagenarians and octogenarians hooked up to the ever-venerable World Wide Web. Inhabitants of Nitt-Witt, you recognized the type of feminine being you desire to occupy a seat on the District 4 Galaxy Council, and that is your rationale behind arriving here today. Be assured that you have my extreme and undying gratitude.

Answer Key
Big Words—Little Meaning, page 88

On Wednesday at 10 AM in the student lounge area, Mindy Wortt and Sammy Yunkova, both eighth graders, broke the school rule of no kissing on school grounds. Unless the two offenders promise to shape up, I recommend severe punishment, including after-school detention with Coach Michowski and picking up trash on school grounds.

Answer Key
It All Depends, Page 90

The principal
Brian's sister, brother or friend
Another student
The janitor

A seven-year-old who lives on a farm

Mrs. Albert, on my way to school this morning I saw a giant chicken playing a sideways piano! No, I'm not telling a fib again. It was a chicken, just like we raise on the farm only big—bigger than Daddy but with more hair on its head.

The chicken was playing a song I heard at my cousin's wedding when I was the flower girl. I got to throw broken flowers all over the floor, and it was neat because none of the grown-ups yelled at me. They just cried.

A talent scout for the circus

Holy smokes, have I got a story for you! Last week I was closing up my traveling circus in the quiet town of Snoozeville, when I saw the most peculiar thing—an ostrich playing an accordion! All the town folk were scared to death of the creature, yet fascinated at the same time.

This ostrich could play "Lady of Spain" better than my lions can jump through burning hoops. The sweet notes, the tune, the skill with which this ostrich played made me weep on the spot. I knew I had to make that ostrich part of my circus. She could make me a lot of money.

I immediately approached the bird and made her an offer I knew she couldn't refuse. Well, this bird must have had her tail feathers in a ruffle because she turned me down cold! She told me she would never consider working for or with a bunch of wild beasts. Can you believe it?

A fourteen-year-old girl who has seen it all

What a dork. I can't believe that ostrich was wearing such cheap sunglasses. Hasn't he ever heard of Oakley? I mean, I guess they were a good shape and all, but how cheap can you get? And when I asked him to play a song by Plastic Chainsaw, he said "Plastic what?" Where has he been? And how about that woman staring at him? Those pearls were definitely fake. How pathetic.

An off-duty detective

I'm not quite sure what that guy was up to, but he definitely wasn't just playing the accordion for some spare change. He sounded too bad for that. Also, he was obviously in disguise. No one can get by me in a phony ostrich get-up.

I have a feeling he was scoping out the bank across the street. I bet the people who were in the café behind him were his buddies. Clever scheme, really. They can sit there pretending to stare at him for hours, and all the while they're examining that bank. I'll have to keep a close eye on this guy.

Answer Key
Who's Talking?, page 92

I woke up, hardly able to breathe. The sun was coming up, so I knew it was early. I tried to roll over, but I felt a huge weight holding me down. The smell of a barnyard filled my room. As I opened one eye, I caught a glimpse of pinkish fur. Just then I heard a snort and a grunt and looked over my shoulder. There, lying on top of me, sound asleep and smiling to itself, was a huge pig that looked like it was dreaming of raw potatoes and leftover pecan pie.

Henry lay there like a hunk of cheese, squashed under the weight of his snoring pet pig. When Henry squirmed in discomfort, the pig became irritated and wondered if Henry knew that pigs need their beauty sleep. When Henry started elbowing it, the pig snorted indignantly and rolled over onto the floor. It wedged itself under the bed and fell back to sleep, once again snoring and smiling to itself as it dreamed of raw potatoes and leftover pecan pie.

Answer Key
Description in Motion, page 94

Angela reaches shakily for the doorknob to the new classroom. As her sweaty palm wraps around the cool metal handle, she hesitates and thinks about returning home, *pronto*. Then she remembers her parents. Not wanting to disappoint them by being a coward, she raises her head high, takes a deep breath and opens the door.

Immediately, Angela is under the scrutiny of 18 pairs of eyes. She looks down at her shoes and notices the canvas is beginning to pull away from the rubber sole. She fidgets with the edges of her books and runs her tongue back and forth over her lips. As she walks with her eyes cast down, Angela sees the edges of desks, the erasers on the ledge of the chalk board, the globe sitting on the floor and lots of pairs of feet. She sighs in discomfort, for she knows that soon she will have to look up.

Answer Key
Keep It Moving, page 96

1. The round faced baby shoved Cheerios into his mouth and drooled onto his bib.
2. When Clarissa casually waltzed in the front door two hours late, her mother's eyeballs bulged with rage.
3. After he slammed the baseball out of the stadium, Bob joyfully trotted around the bases and finally stomped on home plate to score the winning run.
4. The students shuffled their textbooks, sighed loudly and doodled in the margins of their notebook paper while Mr. Donaldson rattled on and on about cumulonimbus clouds.

No one knows what got into Ms. Muckraker that day in the faculty lunch room. Suddenly she stood up and **hurled** a freshly baked pie, **dripping** with fresh, gooey cherries, at Mrs. Hereford. Mrs. Hereford tried to **dodge** the sweet-smelling pie, but it **splattered** right in her face.

Mr. Mealy tried to **scramble** out of the room, but he **slipped** and **tumbled** into a bright purple blob of sticky grape Jell-O. The Jell-O **oozed** out from under him as he **lay** dazed on the floor. He must have **bonked** his head on the cold tile floor, which was now **covered** in a rainbow of pie fillings.

The gym teacher, Mr. Schwarzenmuscles, **trembled** under one of the rough wooden tables and **gobbled** up a creamy chocolate pie as the music teacher, Miss Treble, **aimed** a sticky strawberry tart at the math teacher, Mr. Digits.

The principal **peeked** over the edge of the table, a look of terror in his eyes. Mrs. Shakespeare **yelled** at everyone to stop, but it was too late. A lovely lemon meringue pie **plopped** right on her head, and the tangy concoction **dripped** from her forehead.

Finally the principal bellowed, "Do I have to start **giving** *teachers* detention now, too?"

While his mother was buying fish food at the Pet Palace, Little Hal went around the store opening cages. Before anyone could even blink, the miniature greyhound broke out and raced from the store. When Skip, who was manning the store alone, ran after the dog, all the other pets made their break. The iguana wasted no time waddling into the Gap dressing room next door and scaring a half-dressed 15-year-old girl, who ran screaming into the nearby food court, clutching a huge rugby shirt around her. She tripped over the parade of snakes making their way towards the Mrs. Field's cookie store and landed in the mall fountain.

The snakes were unshaken and continued to slither toward the cookie kiosk. They easily dispersed the crowd of 13 waiting in line. Deathly afraid of snakes, one man hysterically yelped at the top of his lungs. His shrieking immediately set off the mimicking lime green parakeets. While the birds were occupied with their screeching imitation, one tabby tomcat thought it was the perfect opportunity to nail a bird for dinner. However, when he lunged toward the bird, she instantly took flight. This sent the burly tomcat sailing into the big tub of ketchup that Mitzi, the food court monitor, was using to replenish the Heinz bottles. The ketchup tub toppled onto the newly waxed floor.

At that moment, Skip, who was running around the mall herding pets, came around the corner. He slipped on the slick puddle of ketchup and took a head-first dive right into the girls' restroom. Of course, Molly Munroy, the love of his life, was standing there, flabbergasted to see Skip. She burst out laughing, stepped over Skip and left.

After returning the animals to their proper places, the newly unemployed Skip removed the official employee name tag from his Pet Palace polo and went home to nurse his broken heart.

Author and Artist

Randy Larson teaches English, grades 7–12, in Wyoming. *DownWRITE Funny* is his eighth published book. Other Taylor & Francis books by Randy include *Hot Fudge Monday* and *Short and Sweet*.

Judy Larson only recently began cartooning, although she has been drawing all her life. In addition to her illustrating, Judy has taught piano for 25 years.

Married for 23 years, Randy and Judy live on a farm near Burns, Wyoming, with their son, Gabriel, his pony, what seems like hundreds of cats and a flock of sheep. *DownWRITE Funny* is the couple's second collaborative book.

Printed in the United States
by Baker & Taylor Publisher Services